THE PHOENIX OR THE FLAME

THE PHOENIX OR THE FLAME

ESSAYS ON J.K. ROWLING'S ORIGINAL PLANS FOR *HARRY POTTER AND THE ORDER OF THE PHOENIX*

A. IBID

TRL Books

TRL Books
www.trlbooks.com

Cover illustration by Ainsley McGovern.

First edition: February 2025

ISBN 979-8-89766-793-2

To everyone who helped decipher Rowling's handwriting or who contributed an essay. You made this book magical.

Table of Contents

About the Contributors

Louise M. Freeman

Louise M. Freeman is a retired psychology professor who taught at Mary Baldwin University for twenty-three years. A behavioral neuroscientist by training, she received her doctorate from the University of California at Berkeley in 1995. Her interest in *Harry Potter* scholarship began in 2003 when she began reading the books to her children and evolved into a research program on psychology and young adult literature, which has led to multiple peer-reviewed journal articles and book chapters, as well as many presentations at conventions, festivals, podcasts and scholarly conferences. Dr. Freeman writes about *Harry Potter*, *Cormoran Strike* and other popular book series at *The Farting Sofa Faculty Lounge* (www.fartingsofafaculty.blogspot.com). Podcast appearances include *Potterversity*, the *Three Broomsticks*, and *The Strike and Ellacott Files*. Currently, Dr. Freeman works as a licensed behavior analyst and therapeutic consultant.

Alice Arganese

Alice Arganese, a 24-year-old Italian *Harry Potter* expert, has been passionate about this book series since she was a child. In 2021, she graduated in Media and Languages (English and French) with a thesis in English literature about *The Theme of Sacrifice in the Harry Potter Series*. In 2024, she earned a master's degree in Languages and Literatures with a thesis in Sociolinguistics titled *The Dialogic Interaction in Harry Potter: A Corpus Analysis*. In 2020, she joined the staff of the Italian *Harry Potter* fansite *Portus*, where she has analyzed *Harry Potter* chapters on Twitch and organized reading clubs on Discord. In 2020, she also started a *Harry Potter*-related podcast on Spotify. In high school, she even played Muggle Quidditch, and her Beater Buddy became the love of her life. While *Harry Potter* will always be her favorite story, she is also extremely passionate about cinema, television, literature, and music.

Irvin Khaytman

Irvin Khaytman, also known as "hpboy13," is a walking *Harry Potter* encyclopedia from New York City, where he does taxes by day and all things geeky by night. He is the author of *Dumbledore: The Life and Lies*, and has been writing *Harry Potter* essays for *MuggleNet* since 2007 at "The Three Broomsticks". He runs a *Harry Potter* podcast (*Three Broomsticks*), meetup group (*NY Order of the Phoenix*), and dance troupe (*Dancing Death Eaters*). When not reading or discussing books, Irvin can be found dancing to wizard rock or planning costumes for conventions. He identifies as a Ravenpuff.

Asher Scheiner

Asher Scheiner is a social worker, teacher and dad of two from New Jersey. A *Pottermore*-confirmed Ravenclaw, he has spent many hours asking and answering *Harry Potter* questions on many different internet forums under a variety of pseudonyms. He is most proud of his theory on why Hermione actually could have legally freed the house-elves with her hats and is convinced that Rita Skeeter is correct that Dumbledore did indeed kill his sister. He has written about the intersections of *Harry Potter* and Faith, as well of *Harry Potter* and Social Work, for various school projects. This essay is his first formally published work.

Beatrice Groves

Beatrice Groves, Ph.D. and Ravenpuff, is Research Fellow and Lecturer in Renaissance English at Trinity College, Oxford. She has published three monographs, and a wide number of articles on literary allusion from Shakespeare to Rowling. Since publishing *Literary Allusion in Harry Potter* (Routledge, 2017) she has published journal articles on *Harry Potter* and Dickens, Shakespeare and Arthurian myth in *The Use of English* and *The English Review* and contributed chapters on Austen and *Harry Potter* (in *Open at the Close: Literary Essays on Harry Potter*), Snake Women in *Harry Potter* and *Fantastic Beasts* (in *The Ivory Tower, Harry Potter, and Beyond*) and Dracula and *Harry Potter* (in *Potterversity: Essays Exploring the World of Harry Potter*). She guest blogs at *Hogwarts Professor* and *The Strike and Ellacott Files* Blog and has a dedicated blog at *MuggleNet*: "Bathilda's notebook."

John Granger

John Granger, PhD, the "Dean of *Harry Potter* Scholars" per Lev Grossman, has been writing, speaking, and podcasting about the work of J. K. Rowling since 2002 and has been responsible for many of the more important breakthroughs in Rowling Studies, from literary alchemy and Christian symbolism to psychomachia and ring composition. His six books on the subject, his lectures at major universities, and his keynote speaker talks at academic and fan conferences have made John Granger the leading voice in scholarship about the artistry and meaning of Rowling's novels and series for more than twenty years. John blogs at *HogwartsProfessor.com* and hosts a *HogwartsProfessor* subscription site at *Substack.com*, from which platform he podcasts with Nick Jeffery on the *Rowling Studies* program.

Patricio Tarantino

Patricio Tarantino is a J.K. Rowling and *Harry Potter* collector, who created his first *Harry Potter* website back in 2001. Since then, he has been actively participating in the *Harry Potter* fandom with different projects. From 2001 to 2008 he directed Redflu.com, one of the most popular *Harry Potter* websites in Spanish. In 2010 he founded *The Rowling Library*, a fan website focused on *Harry Potter* and J.K. Rowling's other works. With *The Rowling Library* he oversees several projects, such as a monthly magazine and the creation of *The Rowling Index*, a digital archive of everything J.K. Rowling has written through the years. In 2021, he published *The Secret History of the Wizarding Phenomenon*. He lives with his girlfriend Belén and his dog Cappuccina in Buenos Aires, Argentina.

Conventions and Abbreviations

Citations to the *Harry Potter* books will be to book and chapter, not to page number. Thus, for example, a citation to the third chapter of the second book is written as (*Chamber* ch. 3).

J.K. Rowling's manuscripts are individually cited by the manuscript, not the books, websites, documentaries, or exhibitions that they have appeared in.

Interviews with J.K. Rowling are cited in the text by the newspaper or broadcast that they were published in, not the interviewer or interviewee.

The outline for the *Order of the Phoenix* is cited by manuscript version and chapter row. Thus, the row corresponding to the sixth chapter of draft C is written as (Outline C6) or more often as (C6). An appendix at the end of the book provides the text of the outline.

A works cited section follows each essay. A longer bibliography, including a fuller publication history and urls where relevant, can be found in the back of the book.

Abbreviations

Works by Rowling

Stone	*Harry Potter and the Philosopher's Stone.* Bloomsbury, 1997.
Chamber	*Harry Potter and the Chamber of Secrets.* Bloomsbury, 1998.
Azkaban	*Harry Potter and the Prisoner of Azkaban.* Bloomsbury, 1999.
Goblet	*Harry Potter and the Goblet of Fire.* Bloomsbury, 2000.
Phoenix	*Harry Potter and the Order of the Phoenix.* Bloomsbury, 2003.
Prince	*Harry Potter and the Half Blood Prince.* Bloomsbury, 2005.
Hallows	*Harry Potter and the Deathly Hallows.* Bloomsbury, 2007.
Beasts	*Fantastic Beasts and Where to Find Them.* Bloomsbury, 2001.
Quidditch	*Quidditch through the Ages.* Bloomsbury, 2001.
Beedle	*The Tales of Beedle the Bard.* Bloomsbury, 2008.

Introduction

"*Which came first, the phoenix or the flame?*" This question, posed to Harry and Luna towards the end of the final *Harry Potter* book (*Hallows* ch. 29), is the wizarding version of the chicken or the egg philosophical problem, seeking the ultimate origin. The *Harry Potter* books also have a previous state and did not come out of the ether fully formed. J.K. Rowling carefully plotted them, and she revised and elaborated on those plans as she progressed through the series. For the most part, these early notes and outlines have not been released to the public and have not been made available for researchers.

The exception to this is with the fifth book, *The Order of the Phoenix*, where a seven-page manuscript is available, containing a chapter-by-chapter grid. The grid provides a few lines of text tracing each chapter's main plot, as well as some additional attention to a few specific recurring subplots. While some of the pages of this manuscript come from slightly different phases, together they form a complete outline of the fifth *Harry Potter* book as it existed in some early stage in Rowling's writing process.

Using this outline, we can trace the *Phoenix* to the *Flame* and determine how the book evolved. Looking at draft material can show us the difference between a concept that was firm in the author's mind from the beginning and an idea that only came about late in the editing process. We can see what was tried and rejected, and we can gain greater insight into how the author thinks and plots their books, and what their intentions were behind the final text.

Unfortunately, this complete outline, taken as a whole, has received comparatively little attention from fans and scholars. To the extent it has been discussed, most commentary has focused on a single page, which was released a decade prior to the rest, at the height of the *Harry Potter* phenomena. Even that page has rarely been addressed in scholarship.[1] This collection aims to rectify this gap by bringing together new pieces of scholarship centered around Rowling's outline for the fifth book, its relation to the published book, and its significance to the series as a whole. The essays in this collection approach the outline from different angles, but all incorporate it in some form into their analysis.

Context

Rowling has been outlining for most of her writing career. We know that Rowling was already employing some version of outlining during the writing of the first book, though the one example we've seen from that was not a grid, but simply a numbered list of events in chapter seven of that book. By the time that Rowling reached *Goblet*, her outlines had taken up a grid format, but unlike *Phoenix*, they were written in notebooks

[1] See Irvin, "The Missing Halloweens" for a notable exception.

with each "*strand of the story*" as a separate page, instead of as parallel columns:

> *This is the grid for the book that I'm working on at the moment ... This is what I mean about pace. I have to know exactly – even though the reader might not know – when everything happens. You have the month that it's happening so I'm getting the weather right and everything. The chapter title... some of them still to be decided. ... This is one strand of the story, the kind of stuff that has to happen in each chapter. On the back you have more lines with other subplots so you know what's going on. ... I have to fill in some of these as I go, because as I'm writing it occurs to me how and when things will have to happen.* (*60 Minutes*)

Rowling would continue making outlines grids later and still does so for all her *Cormoran Strike* books. Her process has continued to evolve, using color-coded ink for *Lethal White* and then making the switch to digital outline grids a few years later.[2] These evolutions were far in the future, however. When she sat

[2] A page spread from her outline for *The Cuckoo's Calling* was posted to her website in 2016. Two years later, Rowling described her *Lethal White* outline as comprising "*a vast, complicated, colour-coded table showing all the suspects, with blue ink for clues and red ink for red herrings*" ("I plan a lot", *Twitter*). In a 2024 interview, discussing *The Hallmarked* Man, Rowling said "*I used to do everything in notebooks, but increasingly I do a lot of planning ... in tables on my laptop*". She also talked here more generally about her approach, saying that clues in the outline were "*just a reminder of where information is supposed to be given. And different columns for strands of the story. Each row is a chapter*" (*The Sunday Times*).

down to write the outline for *The Order of the Phoenix*, Rowling was still doing this by pen, in one color, on lined paper.

The fourth book was published on July 8th 2000, and in a departure from the quick succession of yearly book releases, the fifth book was not published until July 12th 2003, a little over three years later. During that interval, Rowling did promotion for Book Four, wrote and published two short spin-off books (*Beasts* and *Quidditch*), and was consulted on the production of two film adaptations, several video games, and other merchandise. She also purchased a new home, remarried, gave birth to her second child, and won a drawn out legal battle over an alleged copyright infringement (Tarantino).

The actual timeline of the writing is hard to establish with any precision. Looking at interviews from the time, Rowling says that she had not yet started writing book five when the fourth book released in July 2000 (*Bloomsbury Press*), though she was already thinking about it at the time (*CBBC Newsround, Hot Type*). However, by October of that year she said the book was "*underway*", though "*not very far at all*", and announced the title of *Harry Potter and the Order of the Phoenix* (*Today Show*). She continued to periodically talk about writing it every few months through December 2001 (*Newsday, The Scotsman, Harry Potter and Me*). In September 2002 she said that she had already finished her first draft and was "*revising*" (*CBBC Newsround*). Files preserved by Bloomsbury indicate that the manuscript was delivered in December 2002 (qtd. in Errington 274), by which point the book had already reached the final count of 38 chapters ("Autograph Card Signed").[3]

---

[3] The first of the three outline drafts has 32 chapters. The other two drafts are missing their last page, but would have presumably had 33 or 34 chapters.

Many years later Rowling would state that the outline dates from 2001 or 2002. (Wall text). While we know the book was already "*underway*" at the time of the October 2000 interview, we don't know enough to entirely rule out Rowling's later claim, as it is possible that Rowling began writing the book several months prior to creating the outline, a claim which may be further supported by the close similarity between the first couple of chapters in the outline and their final form.

Physical Description

To date, seven pages from the outlines for *Harry Potter and the Order of the Phoenix* have been published. Based on this material, it seems that J.K. Rowling created three different outlines. The first (A) would have been two or three pages long and was just a list of chapters with a month and a short plot synopsis for each chapter. This was followed by a more detailed outline (B), perhaps two pages long, which added significantly more detail, and introduced columns to track different "*strands of the story.*" This was then more carefully rewritten as a five- or six-page outline (C).

All three versions were written on the same 4-hole punched lined paper. A and C were written in black ink, and B in blue ink.

However, not all three versions have been published in their entirety. C, the final outline, is most complete, with five pages available, covering almost the full book. Only one page each from the earlier A and B outlines are available.[4]

---

[4] It's unclear whether the missing pages still survive, or in some cases if they were even created in the first place. For instance, the final page from A may have only been kept because B and C never got that

The relationship between the seven published pages can be summarized in this chart:

	← Harry Potter and the Order of the Phoenix →				
A					23-32[5]
B			13-24		
C	1-6	7-12	13-18	19-24	25-30

The first page of the seven pages to be released was the blue ink page from draft B. This was shared on J.K. Rowling's website (jkrowling.com) on March 9, 2006.[6]

On October 20, 2017, eleven years after that page was first shared, that page together with six additional pages were exhibited in *Harry Potter: A History of Magic*, first for four months at the British Library in London, and then afterwards in New York City (2018), Kobe (2021), and Tokyo (2022).

In conjunction with the exhibition, several tie-in books, catalogs, eBooks, and documentaries were published which reproduce the seven pages in varying degrees of detail. Of special interest is the catalog published together with the New York exhibition, and the eBook published together with the London exhibition. Those two publications are to-date the highest quality print and digital reproductions available.[7]

---

far. And the surviving page from B is in many places more detailed than its later C version.

[5] Chapters A23-A29 are equivalent to chapters C25-C30. Chapters A30-32 have no equivalent in C.

[6] To access it one needed to solve a puzzle by drawing a lightning bolt. The page remained viewable until that website was redesigned in February 2012 to announce *The Casual Vacancy*.

[7] A more complete accounting of the outline's various publications can be found on page 196 in the bibliography in the back of this book.

Rowling's outlines are constructed like a landscape-oriented grid. The column headers are on the top, and the chapter numbers are on the left. Each row represents one chapter of the book. The first three columns contain metadata: the chapter number, the month the chapter is set in, and the chapter name. Then comes the main column with the plot synopsis. An example of these columns can be seen below for chapter six (C6):

No	Time	Title	Plot
6	Aug	Mrs. Weasley's Worst Fears	The clock – Mrs. W's premonitions of doom – Percy etc – more info + discussion – Ron + Herm prefects – 'Missy' S? – House-elf + Hermione?

The next six columns, seen first in Outline B and C, are for the six specifically tracked subplots. "*Prophecy*" is the main one, covering both Voldemort's plans as well as Harry's dreams. The other five are "*Cho/Ginny*" (the romantic plot with Harry), "*DA*" and "*OP*" (each tracking their respective group, switched in this outline), "*Snape/Harry/Father*" (covering both the revealed information about Harry's father, as well as Occlumency lessons, which played a larger role in the outline), and "*Hagrid+Grawp.*" The exact spelling of these columns as well as their respective order changes from page to page.[8] Most chapter rows do not have an entry for every column. The row

[8] For example, while three pages have *OP* as a column heading, others have "*O.P.*" or "*O of P.*" The column heading with the most variety is the Snape column, which has four different versions observed.

for chapter six (C6) only contained entries for four of these six columns.

Prophecy	Cho/Ginny	DA	Hagrid+ Grawp
Bode is under Imp and under orders to proceed v. cautiously	Ginny here – Ginny/ Hermione/ Tonks	around – Sirius farewell until Xmas	Still with giants

Something that can be immediately noticed from the above example is that Rowling writes in a shorthand, "+" is "*and*", "*v.*" is "*very,*" "*Imp*" is "*Imperious,*" and "*Herm*" is "*Hermione.*"[9] Something not apparent from this example, however, is that this was a working document. Rowling did not have everything figured out prior to writing the outline. Text would get crossed out and replaced either in the midst of writing, or later, sometimes being moved around between chapters. Rowling would also revisit the grid later and scribble additions into the cells wherever there was extra room, often resulting in something that can be hard to read at first. For example, this is how the layout of the Chapter Six Plot column actually looks like. (Boxes have here been added to help distinguish the later additions.)

[9] Throughout this book whenever the outline is quoted, the spelling will be normalized to make it easier to read.

The clock – Mrs. W's
premonitions of doom –
Percy etc – 'Missy'
~~loads of info~~ S ?
Ron+ more info + House-
Herm prefects elf +
discussion Hermione
?

Once deciphered, these grids can be read chapter-by-chapter as a linear outline of the fifth book, offering us insight to the finished book and its creation process.[10]

The Outline

At first glance, especially towards the beginning of the outline, it closely resembles the final published version, though it lacks detail. A reader familiar with the book can immediately spot things they recognize, such as the dementor attack at the beginning (C1), Grimmauld Place (C4), Harry's "*interrogation*" at the Ministry (C5), Umbridge's reign at Hogwarts, Harry's failed romance with Cho, his visions and the Occlumency lessons meant to block them, and Voldemort luring Harry to the ministry to retrieve the prophecy, culminating in Sirius Black's death (A29; C30). Nearly all of the major story beats are present, though they differ in their specifics.

The most noticeable differences are in terminology, chapter titles, and nomenclature. For example, in the outline, the "*Order of the Phoenix*" refers to Harry's student group, while the adult

[10] See Appendix A to read such a linear format of the outline.

organization is called "*Dumbledore's Army*." The term "*firehead*" is used throughout the outline to refer to communication via the Floo Network, likely intended as a shorthand rather than a final, publishable term (B15; C15; C16; C23; C26). Chapter titles differ significantly, sometimes reflecting a change of focus. For instance, "*James Potter's Worst Hour*" (C25) instead of the published "*Snape's Worst Memory*" (ch. 28). At other times they show off new forms of wordplay, such as "*Night Mares*" (C7), referring to the chapter where Harry first sees the Thestrals.[11]

There are also a number of subtle differences in how information is conveyed to characters or to the reader. For instance, Bill is the one who informs the trio that Madam Maxime has returned without Hagrid (B10; C10). Voldemort discovers that only the subject of a prophecy can retrieve it through reconnaissance conducted by Nagini (B14; C14). Harry keeps to himself that he saw Mr. Weasley get attacked (B16; C16). And Umbridge only discovers Harry's DADA group a few months later, when she notices their absence during a quidditch match (B20; C20).[12]

From a plot perspective, the major divergence occurs in the final third of the story, starting with the discovery of the DA, or as it's known in the outline, the Order of the Phoenix. In this version, Dumbledore actually gets arrested and brought to Azkaban, and stays there throughout most of the rest of the book (B23; C23). The mass breakout of Death Eaters from

---

[11] This is echoed again later in the outline with Harry's journey to the Ministry on Threstrals being described as a "*nightmarish flight*" (A26).

[12] In the published book this scene couldn't have happened, as the DA agree at the beginning to avoid Quidditch conflicts (*Phoenix* ch. 16), which may be related to why Rowling switched the plot to them getting overheard in the Hog's Head.

Azkaban doesn't happen until the end of the novel, and the Death Eaters depart from Azkaban directly to the battle in the Ministry, with Dumbledore following a bit behind them "*in hot pursuit*" (C27). The ending of the outline is the roughest and described in the least detail, but it seems that Dementors have a presence in that battle, and Sirius Black meets his demise through them. He is cornered against the veil facing a dementor, and "*chooses death rather than the Dementor*" (A29).[13]

Bellatrix isn't just not involved with Sirius's death in this outline, but she's not mentioned anywhere else either. Lucius (C1; C4; C5), Macnair (C1; B18; C18), and Crabbe (A30) are the only Death Eaters mentioned by name, and Macnair's role in this outline is quite larger than and in contradiction to his role in the published book (C1). Some other characters are absent too, including most notably Luna and Kreacher. A new character named "'*Missy' Slipkiss*" can be seen as well (C2; C4; C6; C16; B16; C17).

While it's easiest to view at the outline as a fixed snapshot, some evolution in Rowling's ideas can also be observed within its composition. One such instance can be seen with Rita. In the earlier outline draft, her only function is to exchange information with Hermione about Bode, to help the trio and reader piece together the mystery (B21). In the final outline draft, this has been replaced with her interviewing and publishing an article in support of Harry, much like the final book (C21; C24).

---

[13] For the readers interested in "in-universe lore", this sequence shows that the veil itself can cause death, and thus lends some strong evidence that in the published novel Bellatrix's curse didn't directly kill Sirius, and that his death was caused by being propelled through the veil.

Another area of internal change can be seen with Harry's dreams. Initially, Rowling planned for these dreams to culminate with Harry actually seeing the prophecy and "*where it is, close up on name, how to get in*" (C27). This concept is echoed in the published novel, when Lucius says, "*The Dark Lord wondered why you didn't come running when he showed you the place where it was hidden in your dreams*" (ch. 35). In the original outline, Harry does indeed act on this alone. However, in a late addition to the third draft of the outline, Rowling adds a note at the end that Harry "*doesn't realise until there that the hall contains prophecies*" (C29). She then introduces a final dream, described as a "*new vision of ? dying in Hall of Prophecies*" (C28). At this stage Rowling had not yet decided that the figure in the dream would be Sirius Black, so there's no mention of Harry attempting to contact Sirius first or of his subsequent capture by Umbridge. Nevertheless, we can see Rowling actively refining the plot and connecting all the pieces.

The outline can also help us understand what Rowling's original plans for the series were when she started versus what she figured out as she went along. Ideas that are present or at least hinted at in the outline are more likely to have been part of her original plan, compared to ideas that cannot be seen there at all. One can also use this outline to look ahead to the future, to the final two books. Here we see Rowling place both Cho and Ginny together in the column which tracks Harry's romantic entanglements, often explicitly playing a scene with Cho to "*contrast Ginny*" (C12). Some of Ginny's moments are muted in the published fifth book, but her existence in that column explicitly shows that Rowling was intentionally laying out the groundwork for Ginny's eventual romance with Harry in the final two books. Likewise, a note in the second chapter of "*Mention of Snape obliquely by Aunt Petunia*" (C2) shows us that

Snape's backstory was being worked on already and that "*that awful boy*" (ch. 2) was always intended to refer to Snape even as originally written.

The Essays

The essays in this book each take a specific angle and look at the outline in more depth. Louise Freeman explores how a combination of specific changes leads to the overall tone of the book becoming more positive, while still maintaining its role as the darkest in the series. Alice Arganese looks at the outline in a broad sense, discussing the differences from the lens of the characters. Irvin Khaytman focuses on Bellatrix Lestrange, why she wasn't in the original outline, and what ultimately necessitated her later addition to the book. Beatrice Groves looks at the swapping of the names of Dumbledore's Army and The Order of the Phoenix, and how this ties into the symbology of the Phoenix. Asher Schiener discusses the relationship between Harry and Dumbledore, arguing that its absence from the outline is an indicator that it was already fully developed beforehand. John Granger argues the other way, that most of the significant development postdates the outline, exploring a complex chiastic structure present within the climax of the published book. Patricio Tarantino rounds off the volume by exploring the outline as a work on its own, demonstrating what it tells us about the fifth book without the hindsight of having already read the published book. The appendices give a more exhaustive guide to using the outline, inviting further research.[14]

---

[14] Appendix A contains a transcript of the final form of the outline with some notes from previous drafts where appropriate. Appendixes

Works Cited

Errington, Philip W. *J.K. Rowling: A Bibliography 1997-2013.* Bloomsbury Academic, 23 Apr. 2015, p. 274.

Harry Potter: A History of Magic. UK ed., E-book ed., Pottermore Publishing, 20 Oct. 2017, pp. 304–07.

Harry Potter: A History of Magic. US ed., Arthur A. Levine Books, 9 Oct. 2018, pp. 240–41.

Khaytman, Irvin [hpboy13]. "The Missing Halloweens – Part 2: 'Order of the Phoenix'." *MuggleNet*, 21 Oct. 2022.

Rowling, J.K. "Autograph Card Signed ('J.K. Rowling') Referring to the Forthcoming Book *Harry Potter and the Order of the Phoenix.*" Partially reproduced in *English Literature, History, Private Press & Children's Books,* Sotheby's, 12 Dec. 2002, lot 517, p. 229.

———. "Chapter 7: The Sorting Hat." Handwritten manuscript outline. *National Portrait Gallery*, exhibited as part of *Beatrix Potter to Harry Potter: Portraits of Children's Writers*, 15 May–26 Aug. 2002.

———. Chapter outline for *The Cuckoo's Calling.* jkrowling.com, 20 Dec. 2016.

———. Chapter outline for *Harry Potter and the Goblet of Fire.* Shown on *60 Minutes*, CBS, 12 Sept. 1999.

———. Interview. *Harry Potter and Me.* BBC, 28 Dec. 2001.

———. Interview. "How I Write." *The Sunday Times*, 5 May 2024, *Culture* magazine, pp. 4–5.

B and C provide charts comparing the chapter names and dates of the outline to the published book, a topic not focused on directly by the essays. The Bibliography opens with a full accounting of the publication history of the manuscript scans.

———. Interview by Evan Solomon. *Hot Type*. CBC Newsworld, 13 July 2000.

———. Interview by Kaitlin Bolger and J.T. Sprague. *Newsday*, 18 Jan. 2001.

———. Interview by Katie Couric. *Today Show*. NBC, 20 Oct. 2000.

———. Interview by Lesley Stahl. *60 Minutes*, CBS, 12 Sept. 1999. Bonus segment "Plotting Potter", released online 25 Oct. 2006.

———. Interview by Lizo Mzimba. "JK Rowling talks about Book Four." *CBBC Newsround*, 8 July 2000.

———. Interview by Lizo Mzimba. "Newsround talks exclusively to J.K. Rowling," *CBBC Newsround*, 19 Sept. 2002.

———. Interview by Stephen Fry. "Launch Day interview aboard the Hogwarts Express." *Bloomsbury Press*, 8 July 2000.

——— [@jk_rowling]. "*I plan a lot. This particular novel's plan comprises a vast, complicated, colour-coded table showing all the suspects, with blue ink for clues and red ink for red herrings.*" *X*, 30 Jan. 2018.

——— [*Published as* Robert Galbraith]. *Lethal White*. Sphere, 2018.

———. "No Writer's Block" *The Scotsman*, p. 13, 9 Aug. 2001, Letters to the Editor.

———. "*These plans date from around 2001/2.*" Wall text for *Planning the Order of the Phoenix*. *Harry Potter: A History of Magic*, 20 Oct. 2017–28 Feb. 2018, British Library. *Printed in Harry Potter: A Journey Through a History of Magic*, British Library, 20 Oct. 2017, p. 128.

Tarantino, Patricio. *Secret History of the Wizarding Phenomenon: How the Harry Potter Books, Movies, Theme Parks, and More Came to Life*. TRL Books, 20 Sept. 2021.

LOUISE M. FREEMAN

From Dark Dementors to Luna's Light

BRIGHTENING A *NIGREDO* THROUGH POSITIVE PSYCHOLOGY

When *Harry Potter and the Order of the Phoenix* was published in 2003, both favorable and unfavorable reviewers agreed: compared to the previous four novels, the storyline had become notably darker, particularly for a children's book. Novelist Stephen King (80) describes the book as "*quite a bit better*" than its predecessors, saying, "*The tone is darker, and this has the unexpected—but very pleasing—effect of making Rowling's wit and playful black humor shine all the brighter.*" Reviewer Tonkin says that *Phoenix* is "*a consistently bad-tempered book, in which our troubled hero runs the gamut of grouchiness from 'growling resentment' to 'white-hot anger' ... Combined with its bulk, this atmosphere makes for a fairly downbeat read.*" Granger calls *Phoenix* "*the darkest and most disturbing of all the Harry Potter novels*" and argues that it is the series' alchemical *nigredo* (or "blackening") volume, as it "*details Harry's near complete dissolution. Every idea he has of himself is taken from him*" ("Literary Alchemy" 38).

Phoenix is also unique in being the only one of the seven *Potter* novels for which Rowling has made some of her original outlines available. Remarkably, these notes suggest a story that was psychologically even darker than the final published novel. The series *nigredo* began as something blacker than black, and not just because of the death of Sirius.

Five specific changes from the outline to the final text contribute to an overall lighter, less downbeat tone. First, the outline more prominently features dementors. They appear at both the beginning and end of the book, and they, rather than Bellatrix Lestrange,[1] are responsible for Sirius Black's death. Second, Luna Lovegood is conspicuously absent from the outline. As her name suggests, Luna is an illuminating light in darkness; she alone gives Harry some comfort after his godfather's death. Third, the outline starts Harry's Occlumency lessons in October rather than January, meaning more unpleasant encounters with Snape and a longer period of failure in that endeavor. Fourth, the outline denies both Dumbledore and the Weasley twins the empowering escapes they had in the finished volume; Dumbledore is imprisoned in Azkaban and the twins are expelled instead of flying to freedom. Finally, rather than having Ron overcome his confidence issues and lead the Quidditch team to victory, the outline has Gryffindor losing the final match and ending the season in defeat. By changing these

[1] For an in-depth look at what Bellatrix's addition to Phoenix means for the novel, see Irvin Khaytman's essay in this volume.

five elements, Rowling shifted the storyline to better exemplify the positive psychology concept of "learned optimism," and therefore promoted Harry's resiliency rather than susceptibility to despair.

What is learned optimism?

Rather than study how to cure pathologies or reduce misery, positive psychology asks, "*What makes life worth living, and how can we build it?*" (Seligman, "Flourish" 232). Positive psychology traces its roots to one of the more negative discoveries of the twentieth century: learned helplessness. Experiments by Seligman and colleagues in the 1960s and 1970s showed that a variety of animals, including humans, after exposure to inescapable adverse stimuli (e.g. shock or loud noise) in one setting, would not attempt escape in later situations. This remained true even if relatively simple actions like jumping over a barrier or moving one's hand could have ended the ordeal. Learned helplessness is now a recognized psychological phenomenon with more than five decades of study, and is useful in understanding both clinical depression and the basic neuroscience of learning (Maier & Seligman).

The opposite phenomenon, learned optimism, would not be described until the early 1990s. From the start of the learned helplessness studies, Seligman noted:

> *One third of the people who came to my laboratory, people to whom inescapable events were given, never became helpless. ... We began to ask the question, what is it that makes some people immune to helplessness? ... It turned out that the key was optimism.* (Seligman, "Flourish" 232)

Optimists, according to Seligman ("Flourish" 234), view shortcomings and failures as, "*temporary, changeable and local;*" this viewpoint allows them to show resilience to the helplessness phenomenon. Despite Harry's emotional turmoil in *Phoenix*, he is, overall, a remarkably resilient character (Provenzano and Heyman), making bibliotherapy with Harry Potter a popular choice for grieving children (Markell and Markell). In the interval between the initial outlines and the final book, Rowling reduced the presence of inescapable dementors and Occlumency lessons while increasing Harry's exposure to successful escapes, sports victories and social support. These changes give the book, and its protagonist, a more optimistic perspective.

Depressing Dementors

Rowling has publicly described the two major inspirations for the dementors of the *Harry Potter* world. Physically, they were inspired by a childhood nightmare, as Rowling explained in a 2021 BBC interview:

> *Their appearance owed everything to a dream I'd had when I was a child that suddenly came back to me. ... I was hiding from a creature that looked just like a dementor: the empty black cloak and the withered hand and it was sort of drifting towards me. It didn't seem to have feet. And, I was terrified and I woke up.* (*The Poet Laureate*)

However, two decades before Rowling revealed the source of the dementors' appearance, she acknowledged that their ability to drain happiness and trigger despair reflected her own experience with clinical depression.

> *It was entirely conscious. And entirely my own experience. Depression is the most unpleasant thing I have ever experienced. It is that absence of being able to envisage that you will ever be cheerful again.* (*The Times*)

In the later BBC interview, Rowling explains that it was "cathartic" to transfigure her illness into a fictional entity:

> *I consciously set out to embody depression. Not because I was trying to tell the world I was depressed. Not because I was trying to write biography. But because we do draw on our own experiences and my experience with depression was a very bad one. ... I wasn't talking about someone who is literally depressed. I was turning depression into a creature, so that was very satisfying.* (*The Poet Laureate*)

Rowling's dementors are a powerful literary representation of clinical depression, with their effects matching all nine of the diagnostic criteria used by mental health professionals (Freeman, "Diagnostic"). While Rowling may not have intended Harry as a literal depressed patient, the flashbacks to his parents' murder that Harry experiences under dementor influence in *Harry Potter and the Prisoner of Azkaban* have been likened to psychiatric symptoms in traumatized children (Sanna). Furthermore, the Patronus Charm, dementor-repelling magic that Harry masters at an unusually young age, resembles cognitive behavior therapy (CBT), the treatment

Rowling credits for treating her own depression (Freeman, "Diagnostic").[2] Specifically, the requirement that the Patronus-caster think of something happy when reciting the incantation is similar to a core CBT principle: reframing negative thoughts as positive ones. Lupin's success in teaching the Patronus charm to Harry is part of the rationale for recommending *Azkaban* as a tool for teaching CBT principles to children and teens (Sinyor et al.).

According to the ring composition model (Granger, "Hogwarts Saga"), *Azkaban* (Book Three) and *Phoenix* (Book Five) are thematically linked by their Sirius Black focus, with Harry's godfather entering his godson's life in *Azkaban* and tragically exiting in *Phoenix*. Had Rowling followed her original outline, the books would have also been connected by the salience of dementors. In the outline, dementors appear not only at the opening segment in Little Whinging (C1), but also at Hogwarts and the final Ministry of Magic battle (A29). This would make the fifth book structurally much closer to the third, where dementors threaten Harry at the school year's start on the Hogwarts Express, mid-year at the Quidditch match, and at the end on the date of Buckbeak's execution (chs. 5, 9, 20).

Dementors were originally brought to Hogwarts in *Azkaban* over Dumbledore's protest, to protect Harry and the rest of the school from escaped prisoner and supposed Death Eater Sirius Black (ch. 4). Even under Black's threat, Dumbledore's dislike for the dementors' cruel methods prompts him to ban them from Hogwarts property (ch. 9). After they attempt to

---

[2] Notably, nineteen years later, when Rowling wrote about a realistic character (Robin Ellacott) who suffered from a literal mental illness (panic attacks), she also had that character be treated successfully with CBT. In fact, Robin characterized other forms of therapy as decidedly unhelpful (*Lethal White*).

administer the Dementor's Kiss to Harry, Cornelius Fudge agrees to Dumbledore's request to remove them from the school (ch. 22).

It is not clear why dementors return to Hogwarts in the *Phoenix* outline. Umbridge was the ministry official who sent the dementors to attack Harry in the Dursley's neighborhood, so it is likely that she ordered them into Hogwarts as High Inquisitor, either over Dumbledore's objections or after his departure. Rowling's first outline describes the students' Thestral journey to the Ministry as a "*nightmarish flight pursued by dementors*" (A26), suggesting that, by book's end, there are multiple dementors roaming the Forbidden Forest, and possibly the Hogwarts grounds itself.

The dementors are even more important at the Ministry fight with the Death Eaters. Rowling's earliest outline reads, "*Harry runs for it with prophecy but Sirius is in trouble—goes back—chucks away the prophecy but Sirius chooses death rather than the dementor*" (A29). While open to interpretation, Sirius appears to tell Harry to take the prophecy and run, as he does in Chapter 35 of the final volume. Harry, rather than Neville, subsequently breaks the prophecy orb, possibly when returning to the veiled archway to assist Sirius during the dementor attack. Cornered, Sirius choses to step through the veil to his death, rather than face the Dementor's Kiss and the loss of his soul. In this version, Sirius's death resembles Dumbledore's choice to die at Snape's hands rather than suffer a prolonged death from the curse in his injured hand (*Hallows* ch. 33).

If anything, Sirius's choice of death in the outline would have been more painful for Harry than it was in the eventual published volume. Not only would Harry bear the blame for being tricked by Voldemort's vision and lured to the Ministry, but, presumably, Harry would have failed to save Sirius with the

Patronus Charm. Harry would have to live with the horrible irony of successfully performing the spell first to drive off hundreds of dementors as a third-year student (*Azkaban* ch. 21), then to save his despised, bullying cousin (*Phoenix* ch. 1; Outline C1), and even to earn a bonus point on his OWLS (*Phoenix* ch. 31), but failing to save his beloved godfather at the Ministry.

In the final manuscript, Sirius confidently laughs as Bellatrix's spell knocks him through the veil, one of multiple deaths that is made more jarring by its juxtaposition to mirth (Freeman, "Ghost of His Last Laugh"). He seems to have no time to process his fate. While tragic, his death is relatively easy, without the excruciatingly difficult decision that was forced in the original outline. Two years later, when summoned by the Resurrection Stone, Sirius is able to assure Harry that death is painless, "*Quicker and easier than falling asleep*" (*Hallows* ch. 34). As devastating as Sirius's death was for Harry, the version in Rowling's original outline appears far worse. Between both the increased self-blame for Sirius's death and the enhanced presence of dark creatures embodying clinical depression, Harry would have been in an even worse emotional state in the aftermath of the battle. At the very least, more of Dumbledore's instruments might have been smashed.

Luna Lights Up the Story

In her original "scribblings" for the first *Harry Potter* novel, Rowling listed forty Hogwarts students. One of them, Lily Moon, was discarded from *Harry Potter and the Philosopher's Stone*, but would later reappear under a new name, after *Lily* was repurposed for Harry's mother. Lily Moon was the "*first intimation of Luna Lovegood*" that "*gave me the idea for a fey, dreamy girl*" ("The Original Forty"). Notably, Luna is absent from all of the original *Phoenix* outlines, but was added to the story in the finished novel, as a strange but appealing fourth-year Ravenclaw who becomes Harry's closest non-Gryffindor student ally.

It can be tempting to characterize Luna as little more than an example of the "Manic Pixie Dream Girl" (MPDG) trope: an original and quirky young woman whose sole role is to present her unique perspective in order to enlighten and loosen up the brooding male hero (Pasola). Harry certainly does plenty of brooding in *Phoenix* and could probably benefit from having such a stock character around. However, there are good reasons to see Luna as moving beyond that stereotype. Fransisca and Mochtar characterize Luna as a nurturer and mentor to Harry, and particularly a source of emotional support. Smith (274-275) emphasizes Luna's purity of heart, saying she upholds a high "*standard of uncompromising truthfulness*" and "*has a quiet but extraordinary integrity about her.*" Luna joins the rest of Harry's inner circle, all "*demonstrating courage, skill, wisdom and humility in their own right,*" and united in the battle against Voldemort (Pasola 159).

Granger ("Literary Alchemy") notes that Luna's name, meaning "moon," is associated with silver light in a night sky and is one of the key identifying elements of the *albedo* (or "whitening") alchemical phase. Physically, Luna resembles both an *albedo* element and a typical MPDG, with her "*long flaxen hair, large silvery eyes and ... unique clothing and accessories*" (Pasola 156). Her absence from the original outline may mean that Rowling originally planned to introduce the character in *Prince*, the major *albedo* work of the series (Granger, "Literary Alchemy"). What, then, does it mean to have this fundamentally good and loving moon-girl introduced in *Phoenix*, the darkest *nigredo* book?

Luna is useful for far more than her familial connections to *The Quibbler* and her Thestral-riding skills. In *Phoenix*, she regularly provides explanations, albeit rather bizarre ones, that shine some light on Harry's murky confusion. Early in *Phoenix*, she assures Harry that he is not going mad and that she, too, can see the Thestrals (ch. 10). While Harry is less than fully reassured, given Luna's other oddities, he takes comfort in the fact that he is not hallucinating alone. Later, he learns (ironically, from Hagrid, who Luna had characterized as a poor teacher) that his and Luna's common ability was the result of an inexplicable, but demonstrably true fact of the magical world: Thestrals are visible only to those who have seen someone die (ch. 21).

There is an echo of this connection at book's end, when Harry and Luna also share the ability to hear the whispering voices behind the veiled archway at the Department of Mysteries. This commonality allows Luna to console Harry following Sirius's death, something Harry's conversations with Ron and Hermione, Hagrid, and Nearly Headless Nick were unable to do. After Luna explains about her own mother dying when Luna was nine, she continues:

> *"And anyway, it's not as though I'll never see Mum again, is it?"*
>
> *"Er – isn't it?" said Harry, uncertainly.*
>
> *She shook her head in disbelief.*
>
> *"Oh, come on, you heard them, just behind the veil, didn't you?"* (*Phoenix* ch. 38)

With Luna's assurance, Harry considers and draws comfort from the possibility that life after death could be like a Thestral: inexplicable but nonetheless real. After this conversation, Harry "*found that the terrible weight in his stomach seemed to have lessened slightly*" (*Phoenix* ch. 38). As Fransisca and Mochtar (5) state, "*No one else, even those who are closer to Harry, understands Harry's emotional turmoil better than Luna.*" This consideration of a spiritual question is consistent with research showing that spirituality is a positive predictive factor for favorable response to depression treatment (Kim, Huh, and Chase, 2015). For Harry, Luna's conviction that even separation from a loved one by death could be a temporary hardship begins his recovery process.

Luna's helping to relieve Harry's despondency in *Phoenix* foreshadows one of her most significant roles in *Harry Potter and the Deathly Hallows*. In a scene that illustrates how both optimism and social support counteract depression, she, with the help of Ernie Macmillan and Seamus Finnegan, support a despairing Harry with their own Patronuses during a dementor attack at the Battle of Hogwarts. After Fred's death and Hagrid's capture, Harry is filled with too much grief and pessimism to perform the spell himself, thinking, "*How many more lay dead that he did not yet know about?*" (*Hallows* ch. 32). Amid the "*dull hopelessness*" consuming Harry, Luna acts as a CBT practitioner would, coaching a patient into transforming negative thoughts to positive ones (Freeman, "Diagnostic").

> *"That's right" said Luna encouragingly, as if they were back in the Room of Requirement and this was simply spell practice for the DA. "That's right, Harry ... come on, think of something happy."*
>
> *"Something happy?" he said, his voice cracked.*

> *"We're all still here," she whispered. "We're still fighting."* (*Hallows* ch. 32)

With this counsel, Harry is able to regroup and summon his own Patronus.

Given Luna's importance in the series resolution, it was wise for Rowling to introduce her in the *nigredo Phoenix* instead waiting until the *albedo Prince*. Her straightforward tendency to speak the truth as she sees it, her courage, and her genuine appreciation for Harry's friendship shine in a way that counteracts the *nigredo* narrative of *Phoenix*. Without Luna's moonlight to illuminate his path, Harry's fifth year journey would have been far darker.

More Onerous Occlumency

Harry's *Phoenix* Occlumency lessons with Snape were one of the most hated activities of his fifth year, a remarkable characterization considering what he endures in Umbridge's detentions. Atypically, he had little success learning this magic: the opposite of his Patronus Charm training with Lupin in *Azkaban* (ch. 12). In Rowling's original outline, Harry begins the Occlumency lessons in mid-October (C11) and continues until early April (C25), a period of over five months, covering fifteen chapters. In the final book, he does not start the lessons until after Christmas, spending less than three months, and only five chapters on Occlumency (chs. 24–28).

The outline's longer duration for Occlumency lessons provides more opportunities not only to fail at the mind-blocking spell, but also to suffer harassment from Snape. For example, the outline describes Snape as "*furious*" that Harry skipped a lesson to go to Hogsmeade (C13), and a "*very bad*

Snape lesson" with Harry failing because of the earlier truancy (C14). Two chapters later, there is a mention of a "*very very bad*" lesson and a row, with Harry "*really in the doghouse*" for seeing visions of Nagini (B16; C16). Snape is later described as "*going ape*" (B20–22) over Harry's poor performance. Although Harry makes some progress by "*starting to get it*" (B23–24; C24) and Snape "*grudgingly approves ish*" (B23–24), that success is quickly followed by Harry's trespass into the Pensieve (C25) and Snape's subsequent suspension of the lessons.

There is little indication that Harry ever "*started to get*" Occlumency in the finished novel, but he does manage to earn some minor approval on two occasions. In the first lesson, after Harry successfully repels Snape with a Stinging Hex, Snape acknowledges, "*Well, for a first attempt that was not as poor as it might have been*" (*Phoenix* ch. 24); while not objectively nice, this comment probably counts as one of the highest compliments Snape has ever given Harry. On the day of Trelawny's dismissal, when Harry manages to penetrate Snape's memories with a Shield Charm, Snape says, "*Well, Potter ... that was certainly an improvement. ... I don't remember telling you to use a Shield Charm, but there is no doubt that it was effective*" (*Phoenix* ch. 26). Overall, the impression is that the Occlumency lessons both lasted longer and were more onerous for Harry in the outline than in the published version.

In early learned helplessness studies in humans, Seligman and colleagues found that impossible mental challenges, like unsolvable anagrams, could induce learned helplessness in the same way that shock and noise could (Maier and Seligman 351). Repeated academic failure can create a helplessness state and reduce students' efforts to succeed in school. Experiments in university students found that repeated criticism of academic work led to students both developing learned helplessness and becoming less motivated to master course material (Ghbari et al.). Harry's longer period of Occlumency failure in the outline would likely increase his helpless tendencies, impairing his performance not just in Snape's lessons but potentially also in other areas of his education. He might even have failed to earn all seven OWLs.

Effortless Escapes Empower

Early studies also found a way of "inoculating" both animals and humans against learned helplessness. Before experiencing the inescapable adversity, the experimental subjects would be allowed to experience successful escapes. Dogs pre-exposed to shock that they could turn off by pressing a button with their snouts were less likely to develop learned helplessness when later placed in a box with inescapable shock (Seligman, "Learned Helplessness"). Learned helplessness can be induced vicariously, by watching others experience inescapable hardship (DeVellis et al.). Therefore, seeing allies escape adversity would be expected to foster resiliency in the observer.

Harry witnesses both Dumbledore and the Weasley twins make dramatic, near-effortless escapes in *Phoenix*. On the night Umbridge discovers Harry and friends in the Room of Requirement, Cornelius Fudge arrives with a team of Aurors and, when Dumbledore takes the blame for creating the clandestine defense group, attempts to arrest the headmaster. Dumbledore is having none of it, responding with full confidence that he has no intention of being imprisoned and, although he could easily break out, he has better things to do with his time. He then knocks out Fudge, Umbridge, and the Aurors with a single spell, and makes his escape with Fawkes, assuring his allies that Fudge would regret his actions. Even the cynical Phineas Nigellus Black portrait is impressed by the ease of Dumbledore's flight, telling Fudge, "*You cannot deny he's got style …*" (*Phoenix* ch. 27).

In Rowling's original outline, Dumbledore is arrested and imprisoned. He is equally flippant about the charges, saying to Fudge, "*Then to Azkaban I must surely go. I trust I am allowed a toothbrush?*" (B23; C23) and he apparently does escape, perhaps during the mass-breakout of the Death Eaters. But, the arrest would have darkened the story's tone and intensified Harry's guilt and distress, given what Harry heard about the horrors of the wizard prison from Hagrid and Sirius in *Azkaban* (chs. 11, 19). As readers learn in later books, Dumbledore carries extensive pain and guilt from his own family trauma, particularly from Ariana's death in the duel with Grindelwald and Aberforth. (*Hallows* ch. 35) Even as the most powerful wizard of his age, he would likely have had some vulnerability when continuously surrounded by dementors, just as he succumbed to the horror of the potion that guarded the locket Horcrux in *Harry Potter and the Half-Blood Prince* (ch. 26). Also, had the Aurors confiscated the Elder Wand, its allegiance might have shifted, complicating Dumbledore's plan for *Hallows*.

The Weasley twins are nowhere near as powerful as Dumbledore, but their final flight from Hogwarts is a similar, nearly effortless escape. Echoing their Beater positions on the Quidditch team as "*a pair of human Bludgers*" (*Stone* ch. 10), Fred and George create a portable swamp in a school hallway, distracting Umbridge so Harry can break into her office (Strand). Umbridge is as eager to punish the twins as Fudge was to arrest Dumbledore, and Filch is positively giddy at the prospect of horse-whipping them.

> *"I've got the form, Headmistress," [Filch] said hoarsely, ... "and I've got the whips waiting ... oh, let me do it now ..."*
>
> *"Very good, Argus," [Umbridge] said. "You two," she went on, gazing down at Fred and George, "are about to learn what happens to wrongdoers in my school."* (*Phoenix* ch. 29)

The twins are as confident as Dumbledore in their ability to escape this trap, and equally adept at making their adversaries look foolish.

> *"You know what?" said Fred. "I don't think we are." He turned to his twin.*
>
> *"George," said Fred, "I think we've outgrown full-time education."*
>
> *"Yeah, I've been feeling that way myself," said George lightly.*
>
> *"Time to test our talents in the real world, d'you reckon?" asked Fred.*
>
> *"Definitely," said George.*
>
> *And before Umbridge could say a word, they raised their wands and said together:*
>
> "Accio Brooms!" (*Phoenix* ch. 29)

Not only do the twins, amid "*tumultuous applause*," manage to soar away on their recovered broomsticks into a "*glorious sunset*," they take the opportunity to advertise their new bricks-and-mortar business to their classmates and persuade Peeves to follow his first-ever order from a student, namely, to give Umbridge hell.

Rowling originally planned to have the Weasley twins expelled, leaving on Umbridge's terms rather than on their own (C26). That would have been a far less inspiring exit, without the cheers that the Great Broom Escape prompted. The twins' flight to freedom was witnessed by the whole school, rather than a small group in Dumbledore's office, making it "*the stuff of Hogwarts legend*" (*Phoenix* ch. 30). It inspires multiple students to either consider leaving themselves ("*One more lesson like that and I might just do a Weasley*" [*Phoenix* ch. 30].) or to vie "*for the newly vacant position of Troublemakers-in-Chief,*" (*Phoenix* ch. 30) by tormenting Umbridge with Dungbombs, Nifflers, and Skiving Snackboxes. Even as Harry is reeling from the loss of both Dumbledore and his underground defense group, and facing distractions such as Grawp, his OWLs and end to his romance, the Umbridge-resistance movement that he had fought (pardon the pun) single-handedly during his "*Detentions with Dolores*" spreads beyond Harry's training group to the wider school, foreshadowing the widespread support that will sustain Harry during the Battle of Hogwarts in *Hallows*. People with strong perceived social support are more optimistic (Chapman and Chi; Tras et al.) and less prone to developing depression (Kaufman et al.). Memories of friends are frequently used to summon Harry's Patronus; similarly, a network of peers, like a history of successful escapes, helps prevent depression (Freeman, "Diagnostic"). Without being able to either observe these empowering escapes, or to appreciate the effects on the student body, Harry would doubtlessly have been more discouraged by the book's end.

Weasley Becomes Quidditch King

Multiple *Potter* scholars see the Quidditch matches as a "text-within-a-text," reflecting the larger storyline. Strand compares Quidditch to Hamlet's staged play, both echoing characters' larger roles and predicting future story elements, concluding that "*a conscientious reader can choose to see a more sublime meaning for Quidditch than what's on the surface*" (Strand 37). Beckoff demonstrates Quidditch's motivational power in Harry's larger mission; it both prompts him to learn the Patronus Charm and comforts him as he faces death. Harper documents how all the series' Quidditch matches point to the larger narrative. For instance, Ginny catching the snitch "*right out from under [Cho's] nose*" (*Phoenix* ch. 31) in the final Gryffindor-Ravenclaw match foreshadows Ginny replacing Cho Chang as Harry's love interest in *Prince*. Harper states:

> *Quidditch serves as both the actual training ground for Harry's heroic actions and the lens through which he sees himself and the world sees him: Chosen One, Seeker, the only one who can end both the game and the "game." From his discovery of both his hidden Quidditch and magical talents to his position as both Seeker and hunter of Horcruxes, his role on the pitch mirrors his role in the Wizarding world's fight against Voldemort.* (Harper 183)

Had Harry relied on Rowling's original finale of the *Phoenix* Quidditch season for encouragement, he would have been out of luck. In the outline, Harry alone, rather than Harry, George and Fred, had been dismissed from the Quidditch team following a November attack on Malfoy (B15; C15). By the time of the Ravenclaw match in May, Fred and George have been expelled. Without those three star players, Gryffindor is "*flattened*" (C27), presumably losing the game and the Quidditch Cup. The outline does not mention Ron becoming Quidditch Keeper, but, if he was, he would not have overcome his nerves for the final game, and the Gryffindors would not have been able to turn Malfoy's taunting "*Weasley is Our King*" song into a counter-weapon against their arch-rivals. Leaving Ron's victory out of *Phoenix* makes his nervousness when playing Keeper in his first *Prince* game (ch. 14) — and his need for the placebo effect of Harry's fake Felix Felicis — more understandable; however, it also eliminates one of few cheerful elements of the end of *Phoenix*.

The Gryffindor victory without Harry as Seeker is an important reflection of Harry's success as a defense instructor. Harper (179) remarks "*Just as Harry has trained the DA to fight after he has gone, there are new members of the Quidditch team who can take his place.*" Moreover, in the original outline, as with Dumbledore and the twins, Harry misses the chance to observe Ron's triumph over hardship and the flipping of the adversary's intimidation tactics into an instrument for ridicule. In the final manuscript, Ron experiences "*euphoria*" in the aftermath of his victory, retelling the tale and evoking a grin from Harry even in the midst of his many other stressors (*Phoenix* ch. 31). Without Ron's triumph as Keeper, Harry loses another opportunity to draw on vicarious victory as a weapon against depression and despair.

Conclusion

In the face of hardship, learned optimists live by the motto: "*It's temporary, it's just this one situation and there is something I can do about it*" (Seligman, "Flourish" 232). By reducing both the presence of dementors and the duration of the Occlumency lessons, Rowling decreased Harry's exposure to aversive stimuli that might have promoted learned helplessness. Changing Dumbledore's, the twins', and the Gryffindor Quidditch team's victimization to empowerment vicariously showed Harry that escape from difficulties was possible, and could even be easy. Finally, adding the odd but unflappable Luna to the Gryffindor quintet of Harry, Ron, Hermione, Ginny and Neville both provided a lighter character for a dark novel and, perhaps most importantly, made it possible for Harry to consider that grief over Sirius's death might be temporary.

With these changes, Rowling crafted her original *Phoenix* outline into a novel that, while still serving as the *nigredo* of her alchemical series (Granger, "Literary Alchemy"), ends on a more positive note. Harry's emotional state and mental health may break down in this book, but the optimistic examples he finds in others set the stage for his later resilience, forming the base for him to develop into "*Dumbledore's man*" who chooses to destroy Horcruxes rather than quest for Hallows. The addition of some brightness to a more downbeat outline recalls Dumbledore's oft-quoted line from the *Azkaban* movie: "*Happiness can be found, even in the darkest of times, if only one remembers to turn on the light.*" As the story from the original *Phoenix* notes evolved into the finished product, Rowling clearly recalled her Lumos spell, and cast it repeatedly.

Works Cited

Beckoff, Laurie. "It's All Fun and Games Until...: Leisurely and Competitive Pursuits in Harry Potter and Chivalric Romance." *Potterversity: Essays Exploring the World of Harry*

Potter, edited by Kathryn McDaniel and Emily Strand, McFarland & Company, Inc., 2024, pp. 179–92.

Chapman, Tracy, and Terry Chi. "Perceived Social Support Mediates the Link Between Optimism and Active Coping." *Journal of Behavioral and Social Sciences*, vol. 4, no. 2, 2017, pp. 57–65.

DeVellis, Robert F., Brenda M. DeVellis, and Charley McCauley. "Vicarious Acquisition of Learned Helplessness." *Journal of Personality and Social Psychology*, vol. 36, no. 8, 1978, pp. 894–99.

Fransisca, Marcelina, and Jenny Mochtar. "The Role of Girls as Mothers in the Harry Potter Series." *k@ta*, vol. 19, no. 1, 2017, pp. 1–7.

Freeman, Louise M. "The Ghost of His Last Laugh: Evolving Humor in Harry Potter." *The Ivory Tower, Harry Potter and Beyond: More Essays on the Works of J.K. Rowling*, edited by Lana. A. Whited, University of Missouri Press, 2023, pp. 133–51.

———. "Harry Potter and the Diagnostic and Statistical Manual: Muggle Disorders in the Wizarding World." *Study & Scrutiny: Research on Young Adult Literature*, vol. 1, no. 1, 2015, pp. 156–214.

Ghbari, Thaer A., Jalal Kayed Damra, and Yahya H. Nassar. "The Effect of Learned Helplessness on Changing Goal Orientation Among Undergraduate Students." *Journal of Institutional Research in South East Asia*, vol. 12, no. 1, 2014, pp. 110–20.

Granger, John. *The Hogwarts Saga as Ring Composition and Ring Cycle*. Unlocking Press, 2010.

———. "The Literary Alchemy of J.K. Rowling." *The Alchemical Harry Potter: Essays on Transfiguration in the Novels of J.K. Rowling*, edited by Anne J. Mamary, McFarland & Company, Inc., 2020, pp. 30–45.

Harry Potter and the Prisoner of Azkaban. Directed by Alfonso Cuarón, Warner Bros., 2004.

Harper, Caitlin Elizabeth. "Quidditch as Narrative Mirror in the Harry Potter Series." *The Ivory Tower, Harry Potter and Beyond: More Essays on the Works of J.K. Rowling*, edited by Lana A. Whited, University of Missouri Press, 2023, pp. 169–84.

Kaufman, Joan, et al. "Social Supports and Serotonin Transporter Genes Moderate Depression in Maltreated Children." *Proceedings of the National Academy of Sciences*, vol. 101, no. 49, 2004, pp. 17136–41.

Kim, H. Y., Huh, H. J. & Chase, J. H. (2015). Effects of religiosity and spirituality on the treatment response in patients with depressive disorders. Comprehensive Psychiatry 60, 26–34.

King, Stephen. "Potter Gold: Stephen King Takes a Shining to J.K. Rowling's Delightfully Dark *Harry Potter and the Order of the Phoenix*." *Entertainment Weekly*, no. 718, 11 July 2003, pp. 80–81.

Maier, Steven F., and Martin E. P. Seligman. "Learned Helplessness at Fifty: Insights from Neuroscience." *Psychological Review*, vol. 123, no. 4, 2016, pp. 349–67.

Markell, Kathryn A., and Marc A. Markell. *The Children Who Lived: Using Harry Potter and Other Fictional Characters to Help Grieving Children and Adolescents*. Routledge, 2008.

Pasola, Kate. "The Integrity of Luna Lovegood: How J.K. Rowling Subverts the 'Magic Pixie Dream Girl' Trope." *Charming and Bewitching: Considering the Harry Potter Series*, edited by S.M. Alegre, Universitat Autonoma de Barcelona, 2014, pp. 153–61.

Provenzano, David, and Richard Heyman. "Harry Potter and the Resilience to Adversity." *The Psychology of Harry Potter: An Unauthorized Examination of the Boy Who Lived*, edited by Neil Mulholland, Smart Pop, 2006, pp. 105–99.

Rowling, J.K. Interview by Ann Treneman. "Harry and Me" *The Times* [London], 30 June 2000, *Times2*, pp. 3–7.

———. Interview by Simon Armitage. *The Poet Laureate Has Gone to His Shed*, extended version, *BBC Sounds*. Originally broadcast on BBC Radio 4, 24 July 2021. Extended version released 24 July 2021.

——— [*Published as* Robert Galbraith]. *Lethal White*. Sphere, 2018.

———. "The Original Forty." *Pottermore*, 15 Aug. 2011.

Sanna, Antonio. "'I Can Touch Him Now:' Harry Potter as a Gothic Narrative of Trauma and Homoerotic Sexual Abuse." *Literary Refractions*, vol. 5, no. 1, 2015, pp. 1–17.

Seligman, Martin. "Flourish: Positive Psychology and Positive Interventions." *The Tanner Lectures on Human Values*, edited by Mark Matheson, vol. 31, 2012, pp. 229–43. Delivered at The University of Michigan, 7 Oct. 2010.

———. "Learned Helplessness." *Annual Review of Medicine*, vol. 23, no. 1, 1972, pp. 407–12.

Sinyor, Mark, et al. "The Boy Who Lived Well: Harry Potter as a Novel Tool for Teaching Cognitive-Behavioural Skills to Youth." *Journal of the American Academy of Child and Adolescent Psychiatry Connect*, vol. 4, no. 2, 2017, pp. 15–21.

Smith, Laura Lee. "Who Deserves the Truth? A Look at Veracity and Mendacity in Harry Potter." *Harry Potter for Nerds II: Essays for Fans, Academics, and Lit Geeks*, edited by Kathryn McDaniel and Travis Prinzi, Unlocking Press, 2015, pp. 271–91.

Strand, Emily. "The Second War Was Won on the Quidditch Pitch of Hogwarts." *Harry Potter for Nerds II: Essays for Fans, Academics, and Lit Geeks*, edited by Kathryn McDaniel and Travis Prinzi, Unlocking Press, 2015, pp. 115–38.

Tonkin, Boyd. "The Boy Hero Becomes Dirty Harry in This Downbeat Read." Review of *Harry Potter and the Order of the Phoenix*, by J.K. Rowling. *The Independent*, no. 5204, 23 June 2003, p. 6.

Tras, Zeliha, Merve Gül Sunbul, and Umay Bilge Baltaci. "Investigation of the Relationship Between Optimism, Perceived Social Support, and Hope." *i.e.: Inquiry in Education*, vol. 13, no. 1, 2021, article 11.

ALICE ARGANESE

From Joyce Umbridge to 'Missy' Slipkiss

HOW THE *HARRY POTTER* CHARACTERS EVOLVED FROM THE OUTLINE TO THE PRINTED BOOK

"*It was about five years to finish the first book and to plot the remaining six books, because they were already plotted before the first book was published*", claimed J.K. Rowling in 1999 (*The Connection*); it has always been clear that one of the most magical ingredients of the *Harry Potter* series has been the author's ability to plan out every step of this complex and extremely detailed story.

One of the most obvious examples of J.K. Rowling's ability to plan out the outline of a book years in advance was released on J.K. Rowling's website in 2006 and later shown in greater detail during an exhibition organized between 2017 and 2018. These very precious documents show the meticulousness demonstrated by the writer in planning out this extraordinarily complex series of novels.

This essay will focus on the comparative analysis between the characters in the published edition of *Harry Potter and the Order of the Phoenix* and its outline. The characters, as J.K. Rowling herself stated, are what *really* makes the *Harry Potter* books such an incredible phenomenon. Reading *Harry Potter* is a narrative experience like no other, but what really creates such a strong bond between the *Harry Potter* series and its fans are the characters. The readers, for example, find in this series of books their ink and paper twins and best friends. The psychological insights of the three-dimensional characters shaped and created by J.K. Rowling are what really allow the reader to experience the narrative adventure *par excellence*: the Aristotelian *mimesis* and *catharsis*.

The complexity of the characters in these novels will be the heart and soul of this essay. By analyzing the characters in *Harry Potter and the Order of the Phoenix* and by comparing their psychology and attitude in the published book to the characters' psychology and attitude in the outline, differences between the two texts emerge.

Missing Characters

Firstly, it has become evident that some characters described in the fifth book are missing in the outline. The most obvious examples are Luna Lovegood, Kreacher and Bellatrix Lestrange.

The Lovegood family was mentioned for the first time in *Harry Potter and the Goblet of Fire*, when Harry and the others are traveling to the Quidditch World Cup (*Goblet* ch. 6). Luna's absence from the fifth book's outline is surprising since J.K. Rowling always showed how much she was looking forward to writing about her. For example, in an interview with Scholastic, the author revealed that one of her favorite moments in the series was "*Luna's first appearance, because I love Luna Lovegood so much and I was looking forward to writing her.*" Her absence from the outline is even stranger when one considers that it is possible to find an initial draft of Luna's character in the description of Lily Moon. The author, in the documentary *Harry Potter and Me*, showed a notebook in which she wrote down the initial list of Harry's classmates and among these students Lily Moon was found (List of students in Harry's year). Years later, on *Pottermore*, she published this complete list, and she commented about this character: "*First intimation of Luna Lovegood, this name was never used, but gave me an idea for a fey, dreamy girl. She was named before I decided on Harry's mother's name*" ("The Original Forty"). Thanks to this piece of information, we know that the writer had been thinking of Luna's personality since the preliminary stages of plotting the series. Despite all this, Luna Lovegood is completely absent from the outline, which makes it quite different from the published edition where Luna is an essential character. Luna's absence is in some way linked to her father's absence. However, even though the Lovegood family is not present in the outline, J.K. Rowling shows that even in these early stages of plotting this book, she was already developing the idea of an alternative newspaper opposed to the *Daily Prophet*. In the outline the author wrote down that "*Rita comes out for Harry in 'The Questioner'*" (C24). This *The Questioner* is clearly the ancestor of Xenophilius's magazine *The Quibbler*.

Another character who seems absent from the outline is Kreacher, who is crucial for the plot of the fifth book. Kreacher is essential for two reasons: he is the main craftsman of the trap that Voldemort sets for Harry by pushing him to go to the Ministry of Magic, and also he saves some heirlooms such as Slytherin's locket. In doing this, he later plays an even more important role in final books. So, if the author had been faithful to these drafts, Kreacher's absence would have had a key impact on the search for the Horcruxes in *Harry Potter and the Deathly Hallows*. Moreover, in the fifth book, Kreacher is the representation in flesh and blood of the difficult relationship between Sirius and his family. *De facto*, Kreacher's absence may be considered one of the reasons why the outline does not focus on the importance of Sirius' gray and complex psychology. In the outline, in fact, Sirius' flaws are not stressed. This means that J.K. Rowling only later thought of showing Sirius, in *Harry Potter and the Order of the Phoenix*, "*as someone who was a case of arrested development*" (*MuggleNet* and *The Leaky Cauldron*). Having said all that, it is important to note that, despite Kreacher's absence from the outline, the drafts mention a "*House-elf and Hermione*" event (C4; C6). This small subplot may be an indicator that the author was already planning to have a House-Elf at Grimmauld Place.

The third main character missing from this outline is Bellatrix Lestrange. Bellatrix's absence is even stranger than Luna's, since Bellatrix herself was mentioned several times in the final chapters of the fourth book (chs. 27, 30, 33). In the fifth book, not only is Bellatrix the picture of the malignancy of Voldemort's followers and the cause for Alice and Frank Longbottom's madness, but she is, above all, Sirius' murderer. Beyond a doubt, if Kreacher's absence from the outline had an impact on Sirius' psychology, Bellatrix's absence from the outline has an impact on Sirius' death. In fact, the main difference between the outline and the published edition regarding Sirius' character is linked to his death. In the book, his death is caused by Bellatrix, while in the outline Sirius chooses to die rather than facing the Dementors (A29). Perhaps, this means that in these early stages, the author wanted to show that Sirius' scars were too deep to be healed. It seems that behind the reasons for Sirius' dramatic gesture are found his sense of guilt towards James and Lily's death and his terrible experience in Azkaban. I believe that these are the reasons that Rowling had in mind when she thought that Sirius would have been capable of choosing to die rather than experience, even for a second, a taste of that mental state in which he had been confined for twelve years.

Apart from Luna, Kreacher and Bellatrix, many other minor characters are absent from the outline, such as Phineas Nigellus Black, Marietta Edgecombe, Willy Widdershins, Mundungus Fletcher, Regulus Black, Graham Montague and most members of the Order of the Phoenix.

Phineas Nigellus Black is not present in the drafts of the fifth book. His absence from the series would have had a strong impact on the last book as well. This would not have been a huge problem, since the author had already planned out a parallel storyline regarding his role in the search for Horcruxes and the sword of Gryffindor; on *Pottermore*, J.K. Rowling explained that in the earliest drafts of the last book, Phineas Nigellus Black was not the one who had to explain the truth about the Sword of Gryffindor to Harry and Hermione, but that instead it was Florean Fortescue:

> *I originally planned Florean to be the conduit for clues that I needed to give Harry during his quest for the*

> *Hallows, which is why I established an acquaintance fairly early on. ... The problem was that when I came to write the key parts of* Deathly Hallows *I decided that Phineas Nigellus Black was a much more satisfactory means of conveying clues.* ("Florean Fortescue")

Marietta Edgecombe is absent from the outline as well. Her absence raises questions regarding how Umbridge discovers the place where Dumbledore's Army hosts their meetings. In the published edition Marietta has a double goal: revealing to Umbridge the truth about Dumbledore's Army and being the straw that breaks the camel's back for the end of the romantic relationship between Cho and Harry. The outline tells a completely different story regarding their romance, because it is said there that Cho and Harry's romance rekindles after Dumbledore's capture (C24). However, despite the absence from the outline of Marietta being the sneak, the idea of a treason behind the discovery of Dumbledore's Army can be seen to have already begun to flash in Rowling's mind, as Chapter 23 of the outline is named "*Treason*", in which the author writes: "*Easter – discovery of Order of the Phoenix*" (B23; C23).[1]

Willy Widdershins is only significant in the fifth novel for the storyline related to the Ministry's corruption. He is not mentioned in the outline, so it can be said that he was later added by the writer because in a book (as *Harry Potter and the Order of the Phoenix*) in which politics plays such an important part, it is useful to have the presence of a character who

[1] In the outline, the Order of the Phoenix was originally named *Dumbledore's Army*, while Dumbledore's Army was originally named *Order of the Phoenix*.

represents the vilest kind of politics' corruption. In the published edition, Willy is the one who informs Umbridge about Dumbledore's Army preliminary meeting in the Hog's Head. However, due to this character's absence, a completely different story is told in the outline, as it is said instead that Harry missing the Gryffindor vs Hufflepuff Quidditch match is the reason for Dolores Umbridge's doubts and the following publication of the Decree Number Twenty-four. Moreover, in the outline Dolores Umbridge herself follows Harry in Hogsmeade.

Mundungus Fletcher is never described in the outline, despite his mention in *Harry Potter and the Chamber of Secrets* (ch. 3) and *Harry Potter and the Goblet of Fire* (chs. 10, 36). If the author had not put this character in the published edition, this would have had an impact on *Harry Potter and the Half-Blood Prince* and on *Harry Potter and the Deathly Hallows*, as in the sixth and seventh novels, Mundungus is a chief character of two essential storylines: the death of Mad-Eye Moody and the quest for Slytherin's locket.

Another character not even described in the outline is Regulus Black, seeing that in the original drafts there are no references to the Black family. In fact, in this draft of *Harry Potter and the Order of the Phoenix*, the author does not underline the importance of Sirius's family at all. This means that in the months that followed the writing of this outline, J.K. Rowling would have had to have plotted out the better part of his entire story; if J.K. Rowling had not taken Regulus' story into consideration, his absence from the last three books would have caused some serious problems regarding the search for the locket of Slytherin, Harry's relationship with Kreacher, and everything Horcrux-related described in the last book.

Montague is a Slytherin Quidditch player, introduced by J.K. Rowling in *Harry Potter and the Prisoner of Azkaban* (ch. 15), who is not present in the original drafts of Book Five. If J.K. Rowling had followed the outline, the absence from it of the storyline related to Fred, George, and Montague in Book Five would have had an impact on Book Six, seeing the importance that the Vanishing Cabinet (discovered by Malfoy thanks to Montague) has in that novel.

In the outline, many members of the Order of the Phoenix are not mentioned as well. The most relevant absent members of the Order of the Phoenix are: Kingsley Shakebolt, Sturgis Podmore, Elphias Doge, Emmeline Vance and Hestia Jones. Kingsley Shakebolt was later added to the book as the perfect antithesis of most Ministry employees to show that even in a corrupted, power-hungry place as the Ministry, integrity and justice can be found. Kingsley plays an important part as a member of the Order of the Phoenix, even in the last novels, and he will become the Minister of Magic at the end of the war. Furthermore, despite Sturgis Podmore's absence from the outline, in the published novel J.K. Rowling uses him as the catalyst of a subplot related to Voldemort's quest to retrieve the prophecy from the Department of Mysteries. Additionally, if the author had eventually followed the outline, Elphias Doge's absence in the fifth book would not have given the reader a sense of rightness when the character is more explored (as Dumbledore's friend) in the last book. Lastly, the absence from the outline of Emmeline Vance (whose death is used as a tool to make the reader more aware of Voldemort's threat at the beginning of Book Six) and Hestia Jones (who will help the Dursleys to go into hiding in the last book) could have been relevant not only in the fifth book, but also in the sixth and seventh novels.

To conclude, other less relevant characters are not mentioned in the outline as well. Some examples: Amelia Bones, Micheal Corner (it seems that his role as Ginny's boyfriend is replaced in the outline by Seamus), Zacharias Smith, Andrew Kirke, Jack Sloper, the Headmasters and Headmistress' portraits, Aberforth Dumbledore, and Rufus Scrimgeour.

Character Names

Another interesting consideration, related to the differences between the outline and the book regarding the characters, concerns the characters' names. Character names have always been essential for J.K. Rowling's writing and plotting, as the author herself stated in 1999: *"Names are really crucial to me. Some of my characters have had eight or nine names before I hit the right one. And for some reason, I just can't move on until I know I've called them the right thing. That's very fundamental to me"* (*The Connection*). For example, in these drafts, Dolores Umbridge is called both Joyce and Elvira Umbridge (C9; B20; C20). However, we don't know why Rowling changed her mind, because when she described the reasons behind Umbridge's names on *Pottermore* she only analyzed Umbridge's final name, Dolores Jane Umbridge.

> *Umbridge's names were carefully chosen. "Dolores" means sorrow, something she undoubtedly inflicts on all around her. "Umbridge" is a play on "umbrage" from the British expression "to take umbrage", meaning offence. Dolores is offended by any challenge to her limited worldview; I felt her surname conveyed the pettiness and rigidity of her character. It is harder to explain "Jane"; it*

simply felt rather smug and neat between her other two names. ("Dolores Umbridge")

Taking a further leap into the past, when Rowling was planning *Harry Potter and the Prisoner of Azkaban*, other names were then being considered for the future DADA professor of Book Five: Mylor Silvanus, Oakden Hobday, and Oakden Hernshaw (Lists of Hogwarts subjects and teachers). It's unclear how well plotted out this character was at the time. In the Book Five outline, however, Professor Umbridge's character is already well plotted out and only misnamed.

Character Psychology

Furthermore, analyzing the characters-related differences between the novel and the outline has given us the chance to explore the dissimilarities in the characters' behavior and psychology between the book and the outline. However, before taking into consideration this part of the essay, it is important to stress that drafts are indeed drafts, so they do not allow an author to fully shape the psychology of a character. Nevertheless, J.K. Rowling, whose greatest ability has always been to create three-dimensional and complex characters, by adding (or not adding) some references to the characters' psychology in these drafts, has enabled us to make a comparison between the outline-characters and the book-characters. The protagonists of Book Five, in fact, behave slightly differently in these documents. The focus here will be on the protagonists:

Harry Potter, Ron Weasley, Hermione Granger, Ginny Weasley and Albus Dumbledore.[2]

Starting with the analysis of Harry Potter, it is important to note that, in the outline, J.K. Rowling sometimes describes Harry as "*very worried*" (C2), yet she does not explicitly mention Harry's anger issues, his disappointment towards Dumbledore[3] and his PTSD;[4] all elements particularly fundamental for the understanding of Harry's psychology in *Harry Potter and the Order of the Phoenix*. Admittedly, in Book Five, Harry's angry behavior towards his two best friends shows the heart and soul of his psychological trauma. In this book, Ron and Hermione are for Harry a sort of "relief valve", as the writer herself pointed out in 2005: "*he has no one else to shout at. ... He's very alone*" (*MuggleNet* and *The Leaky Cauldron*). Moreover, in the outline, no one mocks Harry for what he said after Cedric's death, and Harry's schoolmates such as Seamus and Lavender aren't said to disbelieve in Voldemort's return. It seems that the huge psychological impact of the events described at the end of the fourth book on Harry was not yet plotted out by the writer when she wrote this outline.

Regarding Ron, in these drafts, he is not selected as Keeper for the Gryffindor Quidditch team. In the book, on the other hand, his experience as a Keeper makes the reader more aware than ever of Ron's anxiety and insecurities. The absence in the outline of this storyline means that the writer had not initially

---

[2] The changes in Sirius Black's psychology have already been dealt with in the initial part of this essay, related to his relationship with Kreacher and Bellatrix Lestrange.

[3] The development of Harry's relationship with Dumbledore is explored further in Asher Scheiner's essay in this volume.

[4] Post-traumatic stress disorder (PTSD) is a mental health problem you may develop after experiencing traumatic events.

thought about exploring Ron's weakness and strengths (or perhaps she wanted to dive into this topic through a different narrative device). Additionally, as regards Hermione, in the novel, she plays an even more key role than usual. For instance, she is the one who suggests the DA (*Phoenix* ch. 15), whereas in the outline it is not said where this idea comes from (C12), and she jinxes the parchment that will prevent Marietta from revealing its secrets (ch. 17). She is also the one who pushes Harry to give Occlumency the right importance (chs. 25-30), and then urges Harry to check if Sirius is at home when Harry dreams of him being tortured by Voldemort in the Ministry (ch. 32), a nightmare which did not involve Sirius in the outline (C28). Looking at these differences between the outline and the novel, it is crucial to underline that all these important steps regarding Ron and Hermione's psychology and traits described in the published edition are missing in the outline. So, it seems that in the early drafts of the fifth book, J.K. Rowling did not take into consideration Ron and Hermione's psychological evolution and growth. They play, in the concrete, a less important role in the outline.

Contrary to Harry, Ron, and Hermione, who are less explored, in the outline Ginny's character would have been more explored, so that the imminent romance between Harry and Ginny would have been more explicit. For example, in the book Harry only says to Ginny that he wishes to talk to Sirius (*Phoenix* ch. 29), while in the outline Harry confides to Ginny everything he has seen in the Pensive (C25; C26). Ginny's importance in the outline is surely linked to the fact that J.K. Rowling had planned the romance between Ginny and Harry since the beginning: "*The plan, which I really hope I fulfilled, is that the reader, like Harry, would gradually discover Ginny as pretty much the ideal girl for Harry*" (*MuggleNet* and *The Leaky Cauldron*).

Lastly, as regards to Dumbledore, this character's coldness is one of the main reasons for Harry's frustration in the book, so the absence of this trait would have changed Harry's behavior as well. Moreover, in the outline Dumbledore seems less powerful than in the books because he is sent to Azkaban, and he does not duel against Voldemort. However, reading the outline we can see that Dumbledore's sense of humor remains intact. In one of the few quotations written down by the author in these drafts, Dumbledore would have said: "*Then to Azkaban I must surely go. I trust I am allowed a toothbrush?*" (B23; C23).

Who is Missy Slipkiss?

And now, in the final part of this essay, as Dumbledore says: "*We shall be leaving the firm foundation of fact and journeying together through the murky marshes of memory into thickets of wildest guesswork*" (*Prince* ch. 10). This analysis of the characters, if truth be told, leaves us with a pending issue: "Who is Missy Slipkiss?". In the outline, Missy Slipkiss's actions are described several times, though she is never mentioned in the published book. In the original drafts, this character (whose identity remains unknown) is presented in five chapters; and every time she is introduced as linked to the revealing of information and to the character of Rita Skeeter. For instance, in Chapter Four, J.K. Rowling wrote: "*dinner and masses of information ... 'Missy' Slipkiss*" (C4), in Chapter Sixteen the reader would have found Missy Slipkiss' reaction to Mr Weasley's injury (C16), and again in Chapter Seventeen it is noted that: "*Rita information – 'Missy' Slipkiss bargain struck*" (C17).

It seems that there is a strong connection between Rita Skeeter and Missy Slipkiss. Missy Slipkiss may be an informant of Rita Skeeter's, she may even represent the echo of the protagonist of one of Rowling's ghost plots for *Harry Potter and the Goblet of Fire*, that's to say Mafalda Weasley (see "Mafalda"). I myself would prefer to stress the relationship between Rita Skeeter and 'Missy' Slipkiss. I would like to hazard a guess by saying that this character could also represent the secret hidden identity of Rita Skeeter herself. At the end of Book Four, Hermione pushes Rita not to write articles for an entire year. Perhaps, in the original drafts, J.K. Rowling did not believe that Rita would have kept her promise to Hermione and that she would have published articles under a false name: Missy Slipkiss. This also ties into the name 'Slipkiss' itself, which gives the reader the idea of being caught off guard.

As we have seen, many of the characters evolved throughout the writing of this book, as Rowling wove them together and developed them into the final form we see. If Missy Slipkiss is indeed Rita, then she would join this list of changed characters, though in this case it would be a character arc removed, not added. However, we will only know the truth about Slipkiss if J.K. Rowling herself will reveal it. Who knows, one day she will publish the Scottish Book and maybe we will find out the truth behind the real identity of this character and what plan Rowling had for her in Book Five. But what remains true is the rich tapestry of complex character psychology seen in the book and its effect on the reader.

Works Cited

Rowling, J.K. "Dolores Umbridge." *Pottermore*, 31 Oct. 2014.

———. "Florean Fortescue." *Pottermore*, 5 Dec. 2014.

———. Handwritten list of students in Harry's year. Shown on *Harry Potter and Me*. BBC, 28 Dec. 2001.

———. Handwritten lists of Hogwarts subjects and teachers. Originally published on *J.K. Rowling Official Site*, 9 Mar. 2006 and 31 Oct. 2007. Later included in *Harry Potter: A History of Magic*, British Library, 2017, pp. 124-25.

———. Interview by Billy DiMichele. *Harry Potter: Beyond the Page: A Virtual Author Visit with J.K. Rowling*. Scholastic, Harry Potter Reading Club, 11 Oct. 2012.

———. Interview by Christopher Lydon. *The Connection*. WBUR, 12 Oct. 1999.

———. Interview by Emerson Spartz and Melissa Anelli. "The MuggleNet and Leaky Cauldron Interview with Joanne Kathleen Rowling." *MuggleNet*, 16 July 2005.

———. "Mafalda." Extra Stuff, *J.K. Rowling Official Site*, 15 May 2004.

———. "The Original Forty." *Pottermore*, 15 Aug. 2011.

IRVIN KHAYTMAN

Belated Bellatrix

The Before and After of Advancing the Antagonist's Arrival

If one were to rattle off the most significant antagonists in the *Potter* series, the runner-up slot after Lord Voldemort would belong to none other than Bellatrix Lestrange. The wicked witch seems absolutely indispensable to Harry's story: between killing Sirius Black, teaching Harry about Unforgivables, harboring a Horcrux, and providing an impetus for Neville to evolve, she proves integral to the story. So it's somewhat puzzling that Bellatrix does not make an appearance in Jo's early outline for *Order of the Phoenix*: how could the story have happened without her?

There can be no doubt that Bellatrix would have come to the fore eventually in the series. Her introduction in *Goblet of Fire* was simply too dramatic, and her role as Neville's nemesis too significant, to have never amounted to more than another faceless Death Eater among the Averys and Mulcibers of the organization. In a memory that is ostensibly about both Barty Crouches, Bellatrix steals the scene:

> *The Dark Lord will rise again, Crouch! Throw us into Azkaban, we will wait! He will rise again and will come for us, he will reward us beyond any of his other supporters! We alone were faithful! We alone tried to find him!* (*Goblet* ch. 30)

Every time the Death Eaters come up in *Goblet of Fire*, Bellatrix is specifically mentioned. Sirius refers to her when listing Death Eaters (ch. 27). Voldemort corroborates Bellatrix's words during his resurrection:

> *The Lestranges should stand here. ... They were faithful. They went to Azkaban rather than renounce me ... when Azkaban is broken open, the Lestranges will be honored beyond their dreams.* (*Goblet* ch. 33)

Sure enough, the promised Azkaban breakout comes in *Order of the Phoenix* – Jo had done too much buildup to write otherwise. However, in the original drafts, the breakout was meant to happen in May, immediately preceding the Battle of the Department of Mysteries.

Even with that planned breakout on the books, Bellatrix still had no particular role to play beyond being among the Death Eater forces opposing Harry and his compatriots. The breakout would likely have served as a further extended introduction to Bellatrix, by having her among the ranks of the Death Eaters, and then allowed her to come into her own as an antagonist in the last two books.

We are going to explore what precipitated Bellatrix's earlier arrival and heightened importance in *Order of the Phoenix*, and see how disparate story threads evolved once she did show up.

Wanted: Sirius's Killer

Apart from everything else, the existence of the *Phoenix* outline and the subsequent departures from it illustrate one very important point: Jo is not beholden to her planned chiastic structure when she's trying to tell a good story. We see this in Bellatrix's role in the published *Order of the Phoenix*, when she is nowhere to be seen in *Prisoner of Azkaban*, and in the way Bellatrix replaces elements that were introduced in Book Three and meant to return.

Most dramatically, of course, Sirius was meant to meet his doom at the hands (or mouths) of dementors, rather than dueling his sadistic cousin.

Much as in *Prisoner of Azkaban*, dementors were intended to be an important antagonistic force for Harry to struggle against in Book Five's climax. This is seen in the outline, where Harry's Thestral flight to the Ministry is "*pursued by Dementors*" (A26). This, of course, would also be a callback to the beginning of *Order of the Phoenix*, where Harry has to fight off a dementor in the first chapter (something that is present both in the outline [C1] and in the published book [*Phoenix* ch. 1]). It also would be fitting, in a book where Harry struggles with trauma and feelings of despair, for the dementors to have a large role to play.[1]

More specifically, Sirius and the dementors are closely intertwined throughout the text, as the soul-sucking monsters pursued him throughout Book Three. This intertwined destiny was to reach its conclusion with Sirius's death in Book Five, when "*Sirius is in trouble*" once again from the dementors (Outline A29). Yet unlike Book Three, there is no time-traveling Harry to save him, so "*Sirius chooses death rather than the Dementor*" (A29).

That would have been a powerful ending, and elegant in its parallels to Book Three. We can assume that this was the plan for Sirius for quite some time in the drafting process, because an ominous bit of foreshadowing was left in the published text even after the rest of the plot was excised:

> *Personally, I'd have welcomed a dementor attack. A deadly struggle for my soul would have broken the monotony nicely.* (*Phoenix* ch. 5)

It's a good line to show us both Sirius's humor and his frustration at being cooped up. But imagine how that line would land upon rereads, knowing that Sirius is being glib about the very thing that would cause his death!

The Noble and Most Ancient House of Black

It seems evident that Sirius's familial connections to Bellatrix and the other Blacks were not originally planned. It

[1] For further analysis of the role dementors had to play in Book Five, see Louise Freeman's essay in this volume.

beggars belief that throughout *Prisoner of Azkaban* and *Goblet of Fire*, as Sirius is maligned by anyone and everyone as a seriously bad dude, no one would mention that his brother was also a Death Eater and that his cousin was among Voldemort's favorites.

The outline illustrates just how much of what became the book's climax was still being worked out by Jo when the outline was created. Originally, it was not a vision of Sirius that would lure Harry to the Department of Mysteries – the outline says Harry has "*new vision of ? dying in Hall of Prophecies*" (C28). Since Jo didn't know it would be Sirius at the Hall of Prophecies, there was no trace of Kreacher's treachery in the original outline.

There is a passing mention of a "house-elf" in the Book Five outline, where "*House-elf and Hermione?*" are part of the "plot" in Grimmauld Place (C4; C6). But there is nothing to indicate that Kreacher would play a role in the events of this book, as opposed to being introduced now in anticipation of a significant role in *Deathly Hallows*. It seemed the house-elf in question would merely be part of furthering Hermione's arc as regards SPEW, given that later on "*Hermione wants to incorporate SPEW in Order of the Phoenix*" (C13) – meaning, of course, the student group that'd later be renamed the DA.

In fact, so much of Sirius's character arc in *Order of the Phoenix* is nowhere to be seen in the outline. When we think of Sirius Black, especially in connection to Book Five, almost the first thing that jumps to mind is his unhappiness at being cooped up in Grimmauld Place. His angst about it in *Order of the Phoenix* – as a way of relating to Harry's angst, as a way of decimating his reliability as a mentor, and as a lead-in to his untimely end – is his defining aspect. Yet in the outline, there is zero mention of Sirius being angsty or unhappy – or even being trapped at Grimmauld Place at all.

The final version of the book is so much stronger for having the tragedy of Sirius Black. He is a man who was imprisoned for twelve years, broke out and went through hell to get his freedom, only to end up a prisoner once more. Once Jo landed on that arc, I think she began fleshing out the things that Sirius would find so onerous: a family he disagreed with and loathed, a house-elf who'd internalized all of the abhorrent family creed, and a house where both were inescapable.

Once that became Sirius's story, Jo found a much more satisfying way of having Sirius meet his doom. If his arc is about his antipathy towards his family, why not have that family be his undoing? I'm guessing that's when Jo landed on the brilliant change to have Bellatrix be both Sirius's cousin and his murderer. In one fell swoop, Bellatrix becomes a powerful and loathed adversary, and provides a Shakespearean end to Sirius's tragedy, where he is killed by an embodiment of the very thing he loathed and struggled against. It seems worth it to scupper the Sirius-dementor connection to give Sirius such a catastrophic ending, and to give Harry and the reader an immediate and personal reason to hate Bellatrix.

Kreacher's indirect role in this tragedy is merely the cherry on top. Similarly, looping in Narcissa further drives home that point, and also creates a harbinger of her upcoming prominence in the last two books. But I think the heart of Sirius's struggle against the Blacks is in making Bellatrix his cousin and his undoing. Depending on how much emphasis Jo placed on Sirius's evolved story arc, maybe it was only once Bellatrix became a cousin that she was given the role of killing Sirius.

The Other Death Eater

Aside from dementors, the outline contained another chiastic throwback to *Prisoner of Azkaban* in terms of antagonists. It was the return of Book Three's tertiary antagonist: Walden Macnair. Like with Bellatrix, Jo did some work in establishing Macnair as a Death Eater in *Goblet of Fire*: Voldemort mentions him during his resurrection (*Goblet* ch. 33).

In the original outline of Book Five, Macnair had a much bigger role to play – to the extent he shows up twice in the outline, whereas he wouldn't really merit a mention in an outline of the published version. First, he is "*casing joint*" regarding the prophecy with Lucius Malfoy at the very beginning (C1); second, he is the one to kill Bode in December given that he's seen visiting Bode at St. Mungo's (B18; C18).

It makes sense for Macnair to have a somewhat prominent role, given Book Five is all about infiltrating the Ministry and Macnair works there. He serves as an example of the Respectables, Death Eaters who stayed out of Azkaban and are now parlaying their status in society to Voldemort's advantage. He also vividly displays how bad things are at the Ministry, when they have a Death Eater in a job where he can act out all his violent impulses. Lastly, Jo doesn't have to do legwork in introducing him to us, we already know and dislike him from *Prisoner of Azkaban*.

But for all that Macnair is useful to the plot, and to illustrating aspects of wizarding society, he is distinctly uninteresting as a character. As Dumbledore puts it, Macnair is among "*the thuggish, gravitating toward a leader who could show them more refined forms of cruelty*" (*Prince* ch. 17). The executioner is yet another violent thug, who is made largely redundant by Lucius Malfoy as a Respectable Death Eater who's a conduit to the Ministry of Magic. Perhaps Jo had grander plans for Macnair once upon a time, but more likely he was meant to be a regular Death Eater, one whom the plot wouldn't miss. Small wonder he ended up shipped off to the giants in the published book.

So all of this begs the question: why, and in what order, did Bellatrix's rise to prominence get moved up in *Order of the Phoenix*, seemingly at the expense of Macnair's role? We've established that there was a satisfying alternative in place for Bellatrix's role in killing Sirius. Jo could have added color to Voldemort's ranks with Macnair instead of Bellatrix, even if it wasn't as vibrant an option. So we look to the one final role that Bellatrix had to play in Book Five, one that there was no good alternative for.

Transforming Neville

Neville Longbottom was always meant to play a part in the story of *Harry Potter*, going back to the very first book and his small but significant role in the climax. His specific arc, with Bellatrix as his nemesis, was established in *Goblet of Fire* with the revelation of his parents' fate. And his transformation from bumbling classmate to worthy ally was meant to happen in Book Five, because even in the outline we see his two biggest story beats present: encountering him and his family at St. Mungo's (B18; C18), and Neville partaking in the Battle of the Department of Mysteries ("*[Thestral] horses and Neville and Ginny*" [C28]). These then nicely set up the revelation that Neville was the also-ran of the prophecy (A31) – by which point he's an important character rather than one among Harry's classmates.

If Neville is partaking in battles against Death Eaters, he needed to have a pronounced transformation. Unless, perhaps, the original plan was for him to be present yet totally inept; if it was, then Jo thought better of it. Perhaps the plan was for Bellatrix to motivate Neville to become a badass after the fifth book and Jo moved it up; or perhaps Neville's growth was originally planned without much thought given to the immediate motivation. Regardless, once Jo sat down to write it, the answer must have been obvious: the way to precipitate Neville's transformation is for Bellatrix Lestrange to re-enter the scene:

> *Harry was pleased to see that all of them ... had been spurred on to work harder than ever by the news that ten more Death Eaters were now on the loose, but in nobody was this improvement more pronounced than in Neville. The news of his parents' attackers' escape had wrought a strange and even slightly alarming change in him. He had not once mentioned his meeting with Harry, Ron and Hermione on the closed ward in St Mungo's and, taking their lead from him, they had kept quiet about it too. Nor had he said anything on the subject of Bellatrix and her fellow torturers' escape. In fact, Neville barely spoke during the DA meetings any more, but worked relentlessly on every new jinx and counter-curse Harry taught them, his plump face screwed up in concentration, apparently indifferent to injuries or accidents and working harder than anyone else in the room. He was improving so fast it was quite unnerving and when Harry taught them the Shield Charm ... only Hermione*

> *mastered the charm faster than Neville.* (*Phoenix* ch. 25)

I believe it was this passage, rather than any other, that required a recalibration of the story to bring Bellatrix into prominence. And we can reverse-engineer the adjustments this would have made to Jo's original outline, to see how it resulted in the tome we have on our bookshelves.

If Neville needs to be motivated by Bellatrix's re-emergence, the Azkaban breakout needs to be moved way earlier in the year, rather than immediately preceding the Battle of the Department of Mysteries. Once that chronological shift happened, Neville wasn't the only one impacted by it – so were plenty of other characters.

Rita and Rookwood

There were two antagonists introduced in *Goblet of Fire* whose return in the fifth book was dramatically altered by the earlier Azkaban breakout.

Moving the Azkaban breakout to the middle of the book allows for a tightening of Rita Skeeter's part in the story. Originally, Rita Skeeter was meant to be a recurring character throughout Book Five. Hermione would initially contact her in November, after Nagini's attack on Mr. Weasley (Outline B16; C16), and the initial meeting would be in December, in the chapter "*Rita Returns*" (B17; C17).[2] Then Rita would reappear after a disastrous Valentine's Day (B21; C21), publish the pro-Harry article in April (C24), and still factor into the plot after

[2] Can we just be thankful that we got both a spectacular title ("The Beetle at Bay") and one of the series' funniest scenes thanks to the changes in the story?

the Azkaban Breakout (where her name appears: "*Azkaban breakout – Rita*" [C27]).

As much fun as it would be to have Rita recur throughout the book, a more focused appearance makes sense. Neville is not the only one who's motivated by the earlier Azkaban breakout; it also spurs Hermione to take action and make overtures to Rita. That sets the stage for a more believable opening in Harry's public relations battle against the Ministry:

> *[T]he speakers were not satisfied with the* Prophet*'s version of how and why ten Death Eaters had managed to break out of the Azkaban fortress. In their confusion and fear, these doubters now seemed to be turning to the only other explanation available to them: the one that Harry and Dumbledore had been expounding since the previous year.* (*Phoenix* ch. 25)

Without that inciting incident, for all that Rita would support Harry in *The Quibbler* or *The Questioner*, why would readers believe that over the *Daily Prophet*'s party line?

Furthermore, moving the Azkaban breakout earlier in the year allows Jo to avail herself of the other Death Eaters who were in Azkaban. Among their numbers is the helpfully established Augustus Rookwood – per *Goblet of Fire*, "*Augustus Rookwood of the Department of Mysteries*" (ch. 30) – who was sold out to Azkaban by Karkaroff. Given that Voldemort is obsessed with getting into said Department of Mysteries, Rookwood's freedom earlier on allows him to provide Voldemort with crucial information about the Ministry, as we see him do (*Phoenix* ch. 26).

Rookwood's newfound role would have spelled the death knell for any prominence Macnair enjoyed in the book.

Between Rookwood's much more direct connection to the area of interest, and Lucius's overall prominence in the series, Macnair was left redundant as a source of Ministry intelligence. And if he didn't have much to do Ministry-wise, he could be excluded from Bode and St. Mungo's as well, and reduced to a brief mention *vis-à-vis* the giants. So it wasn't actually Bellatrix who replaced Macnair's specific Death Eater role, but Rookwood – Bellatrix was just the one who made it happen by necessitating an Azkaban breakout.

Too Much Fun

While there are good plot-related and character-development-related reasons to bring Bellatrix to the fore, we should not discount another consideration: she was just a lot of fun for Jo to write. Perhaps once Jo had Bellatrix in a scene at the Department of Mysteries, she couldn't resist writing more of the batty Death Eater.

While Jo has never, to my knowledge, spoken about how much she enjoys writing Bellatrix, she has gone on record with how much she enjoys writing the other sadistic witch introduced in *Order of the Phoenix*: Dolores Umbridge.

Jo has explicitly drawn the connection between Umbridge and Bellatrix. In the *Pottermore* piece on Umbridge, Jo noted, "*[Umbridge] actively enjoys subjugating and humiliating others, and except in their declared allegiances, there is little to choose between her and Bellatrix Lestrange*" ("Dolores Umbridge").

Jo also spoke to how much she enjoys writing Umbridge. Umbridge came up in Melissa Anelli's and Emerson Spartz's interview with Jo immediately following the release of Book Six.

Melissa: Are we going to see more of her?

[Jo nods]

Melissa: You say that with an evil nod.

Jo: Yeah, it's too much fun to torture her not to have another little bit more before I finish. (*MuggleNet* and *The Leaky Cauldron*)

So Jo likes writing about Umbridge, and she thinks Umbridge and Bellatrix are alike in important ways – we can extrapolate with the transitive property that Jo would enjoy writing Bellatrix Lestrange as a character. (It certainly comes off that way on the page!) So it doesn't seem a stretch to think that after Jo had gotten a grasp on Umbridge while writing Book Five, and gotten a taste of Bellatrix's energy in a scene, she decided to go all in on Book Five highlighting sadistic witches who like hurting children. Maybe all the ways Bellatrix's presence improved the story are just happy byproducts of Jo letting an interesting character take prominence.

The Shadow of the Series

There's one final reason why it served the series to introduce Bellatrix earlier on, and it's more of a big-picture item than looking at the nitty-gritty of plot beats.

Bellatrix serves as the antithesis of the supreme virtue in the *Harry Potter* series: maternal love. She's the only married woman we see in the series who, rather than focusing on family, prioritizes something else (in this case, her obsession with Voldemort and her advancement as a Death Eater).

The *Potter* series was clearly informed by Jo's relationship to her own late mother, which is what makes a mother's love the most powerful and virtuous force in the series. Bellatrix spices things up by serving as the shadow archetype, a woman who doesn't have children and actively enjoys hurting them. We know this is the aspect of Bellatrix that Jo was always focused on, because Jo always intended for Bellatrix to be taken down by her opposite, Molly Weasley:

> *I always knew Molly was going to finish her off. ... It was the meeting of two kinds of – if you call what Bellatrix feels for Voldemort love, I guess we'll call it love, she has a kind of obsession with him, it's a very sick obsession ... and I wanted to match that kind of obsession with maternal love... the power that you give someone by loving them. So Molly was really an amazing exemplar of maternal love. ... There was something very satisfying about putting those two women together.* (Carnegie Hall)

Given Bellatrix's thematic importance to the series, it only makes sense to introduce her earlier in Book Five, so she can be a full-fledged antagonist for several books before meeting her end at Mrs. Weasley's wand.

Just as Molly Weasley was always meant to be the cause of Bellatrix's demise, I believe that Narcissa Malfoy was always meant to be Bellatrix's sister – from way before they became cousins of Sirius Black. Narcissa's pivotal role in the series climax, with its parallelism to Lily Potter, and leading to a further parallel between Draco and Harry, was almost certainly planned from very early on. So since Narcissa was to be an avatar of maternal love that would bookend the series, how poetic is it to make her opposite in that – Bellatrix – her actual sister?[3]

Making Bellatrix and Narcissa sisters was inspired, since Bellatrix is literally the shadow image of Narcissa – "*dark as her sister was fair*" (*Prince* ch. 2). Bellatrix states outright, "*If I had sons, I would be glad to give them up to the service of the Dark Lord!*" (*Prince* ch. 2). Whereas Narcissa sells out the Dark Lord to save her son. While Molly, due to proximity, is the opposite of Bellatrix that's emphasized at the end of *Deathly Hallows*, I believe Narcissa was meant to serve as an equally vivid contrast, due to the two witches' sororal bond.

The Best Lieutenant

While Voldemort is a fearsome villain all on his own, he becomes even more so when he has impressive underlings whom Harry and co. can face off against. The most impressive of the Death Eaters, Barty Crouch Junior, was out of commission after *Goblet of Fire*.[4] Lucius Malfoy, if one considers him impressive, had to be removed from action after Book Five to allow Draco his character arc. Give or take Snape and his murky loyalties, who would be an impressive Death Eater in the last two books rather than serving as a grunt?

Bellatrix was the obvious choice for the role, as had been foreshadowed in *Goblet of Fire*. But she is so much more effective as Voldemort's "*last, best lieutenant*" (*Hallows* ch. 36)

---

[3] We should also note that making Bellatrix and Narcissa sisters allows Bellatrix to serve as a malevolent influence on Draco once Lucius is shipped off to Azkaban, which may be of understated importance to Draco's evolution in the last two books.

[4] I argue because he was *too* formidable, and Harry just wouldn't be able to plausibly best him.

thanks to the starring role Jo gave her in *Order of the Phoenix* – I think Jo definitely made some very good choices when she deviated from her outline to usher in Bellatrix Lestrange as an antagonist.

If we are right in how Bellatrix's role precipitated all kinds of changes in the fifth book – Sirius's family resentment and death, Rita Skeeter's more focused appearance, and Macnair's demotion to a giant envoy – then I'm grateful that Bellatrix captured Jo's imagination the same way she's captured ours. *Order of the Phoenix* is a much better book for it.

Works Cited

Rowling, J.K. "Dolores Umbridge." *Pottermore*, 31 Oct. 2014.

———. Interview. "J.K. Rowling Open Book Tour". Carnegie Hall, New York City, 19 Oct. 2007.

———. Interview by Emerson Spartz and Melissa Anelli. "The MuggleNet and Leaky Cauldron Interview with Joanne Kathleen Rowling." *MuggleNet*, 16 July 2005.

ASHER SCHEINER

Angry Harry Potter and the Pointless Prophecy

WHY THE MOST ANNOYING PARTS OF *ORDER OF THE PHOENIX* ARE INTENTIONAL (AND HOW THE OUTLINE SHOWS US THIS)

After J.K. Rowling first released some notes of a rough outline of *Harry Potter and the Order of the Phoenix*, die-hard fans had a field day going through it and cataloging differences between the outline and the final published book. Many people took great interest in how the names of Dumbledore's Army and Order of the Phoenix were originally swapped, how Luna Lovegood is entirely absent from those notes, and how Dumbledore was originally supposed to be imprisoned in Azkaban. But when more of the outline[1] later became available, the part that most intrigued me was just two words, both of them "*Dumbledore*" (C10; A30). Most of the other aspects of the outline were coupled with some explanatory text, for example: "*Ginny – cheeky and funny*" (C4); "*Snape not present – hint why*" (C4); "*Hagrid still with giants*" (C7). However, in two places, the outlines for what were once chapters 10 and 30, the word "*Dumbledore*" stands alone, almost naked, with no explanatory text. I wondered as to what events these referred and to why J.K. Rowling omitted those events. After a careful analysis, I came to the conclusion that these two "*Dumbledore*"s hold a hint to a solution to one of the greatest mysteries and frustrations of the original series: What was J.K. Rowling's primary point and purpose of the plot of *Order of the Phoenix*, and what was the purpose of *Order of the Phoenix*'s plotline in the series as a whole?[2]

It is no secret that *Phoenix* is constantly rated one of the series' least liked books.[3] There are two primary reasons one can find online for this. The first is that the book is depressing. Melissa Anelli of *The Leaky Cauldron*, in her book *Harry, a History* describes how she felt reading *Phoenix* for the first time:

---

[1] I use *outline* for the published grid outline of *Phoenix*, and I use *original plan* for Rowling's supposed first outline of the series as a whole.

[2] I use *plot* to describe the internal storyline of an individual book like *Phoenix* (as distinct from the early outline manuscript of it) and *plotline* to describe the series storyline of all seven books.

[3] It shares this distinction with *Chamber of Secrets*. This is the general impression I get browsing Reddit (see "What's your least favorite") and other fan sites. For what it's worth, Spartz and Mugglenet in their *Harry Potter Should Have Died* (150) also rate *Phoenix* as the worst book, slightly worse than *Chamber of Secrets*.

"*[Harry] had turned into someone I had little interest in spending eight hundred more pages with. ... it was as though dementors had sucked the happiness out of the book*" (163). She's not the only one who feels this way. Emerson Spartz of *Mugglenet* also rates *Phoenix* as the worst book, calling it "*depressing*" and "*a real downer*" (Spartz and Schoen 147).

The second reason the book is disliked is that *Phoenix* seemingly does little to advance the series plotline as a whole. Emerson Spartz calls it "*the worst anticlimax in the series*" (148). Both Dumbledore's Army and the Order of the Phoenix as a concept play little to no role in the final battle of *Deathly Hallows*. Voldemort merely reveals himself again (something that could have been done at the end of *Goblet of Fire* with little damage to the main plotline, saving us upwards of eight hundred pages), and *Phoenix*'s primary plot, the prophecy that Dumbledore tried to hide from Harry and Voldemort all these years, ends up being primarily a MacGuffin — there to drive the plot along but revealing no new information — as we already knew that Harry had to be the one to kill Voldemort!

A comment on Reddit puts it best:

> *As a kid, after I read the book for the first time, I remember asking my friends what the "big weapon" was and was very disappointed to learn it was just the prophecy. Especially since them trying to kill each other seemed like the foregone conclusion for the finale of the books. Voldemort had already heard half of the prophecy and it doesn't seem like not hearing the rest altered his "kill Harry" plan. Overall, the 5th book didn't move the plot of the series along much. I kind of think she didn't have any better ideas but it was too late to change the one*

school year equals one book format. ("In OOTP, Why Is It So Important", *Reddit*)

However, after seeing the words "Dumbledore", without any other explanatory gloss, I think that this perception is wrong. J.K. Rowling had a very specific idea what *Phoenix*'s plot was for and what its relationship was to the larger series plotline, and she succeeded admirably. Let me explain.

J.K. Rowling claims that "*From the start I knew there would be seven books and I had the whole story plotted out early on. It took me five years to write the first book in the series, Harry Potter and the Philosopher's Stone*" ("My Story"). This strongly suggests that the basic series plotline had already been sketched out before the first book was published. Yet there is no question that certain major elements from the plotline did not yet exist at the time the book was first published. For example, I strongly believe that the entire subplot of Snape and Harry's mom is a later retcon and did not yet exist in Rowling's mind when the first book was written.[4] It also seems likely that the concept of a Horcrux was a later invention that was retconned to fit the similar diary. And of course, characters such as Luna Lovegood are such late inventions that they don't even exist in the discovered *Phoenix* outline! (There were also concepts that

---

[4] In *Stone*, Snape seems to be an average wizard who needs Mr. Filch's (of all people!) help to bandage his legs. He simply seems to be merely a standard "evil teacher" that is commonplace for British boarding school books. He saves Harry so he can "*curse [Harry's] father's memory in peace*" (*Stone* 17). Contrast that to the later books, where Snape will become the third most powerful wizard in Britain with a powerful long-dead love.

seem to have been abandoned, such as life debts.[5]) In contrast, the Harry vs Voldemort subplot is carefully crafted through all seven books leading to a final battle where Harry defeats Voldemort via dying, the same way his mom died to save him. That seems likely to have existed in Rowling's original plan.

We can speculate that Rowling had originally worked out a plan where the primary purpose of each book was clearly indicated for the series as a whole. Unfortunately, there's no way to confirm what parts were in that plan, but if we can find a hint, we can assume that those parts are what Rowling's primary purpose in *Phoenix* was. Which brings us to J.K. Rowling's discovered outline for *Phoenix* and the two mentions of "*Dumbledore*" which oddly lack an explanatory gloss.

Here is where we get into speculative territory: The lack of an explanatory gloss has a specific meaning, which we can learn from lexicography. The founder of *Wordnik*, a startup trying to find the "*million missing words of English,*" describes in an interview to the New York Times how they determine when exactly a word enters the language: "*We can actually measure when words get adopted in mainstream lingo by looking at when writers stop explaining neologisms like 'infotainment'*[6] *and start using them as if their meanings were commonly understood*" (Singer). The same process is used by dictionary editors when determining the date when a foreign word has fully entered English: When it starts regularly lacking an explanatory gloss, it is considered fully English and will then be added to the English dictionary (Stamper 82).

---

[5] For an interesting discussion of life debts see Spartz, et al. (86–95).

[6] For example, a gloss on the word infotainment would look like this: "Infotainment, a portmanteau of information and entertainment".

A similar thought process is used by scholars in determining the age of Jewish oral law, like the Mishna or Halacha. Paradoxically, in general, the oldest dated Jewish law writings deal with rare or unusual cases, while everyday law was not codified until much later, simply because it was so familiar it was unnecessary to commit it to writing. In contrast, it was the unusual cases that needed to be written down because otherwise they'd be forgotten (Taub 176). This is why in the *Mishna*, the earliest strata deal with Temple Law, because it needed to be written down after the destruction of the temple to prevent forgetting (see Brody).

Similarly, one can reasonably conclude that those elements within the outline that are without a gloss are older elements of the book's plot or series plotline. Those parts are "set in stone" in Rowling's mind and thus need no explanation. Only the parts that need to be etched out and explained or recalled require more elaboration. This theory actually matches what we know about the *Phoenix* outline: The last version of the outlines we possess omits details that make it into the book which do appear in an earlier outline, presumably because Rowling already had them set in her mind and thus had no need to reoutline them![7] We can then deduce when Rowling writes just "*Dumbledore*" in the outline, that implies she already had something set in mind that did not need to be committed to writing. Furthermore, the very fact that it is not elaborated — in contrast to almost all

[7] In Outline A, Rowling details a "*death room*" and "*love room*" seen in the ministry (A27), which are shortened in the later Outline C as "*death — love*" (C29), omitting the room detail, as the context, while unclear to us, is clear to Rowling. Outline A further includes in detail them arriving and fighting through the ministry (A26), all of which make it to the final book (ch. 34-35). Outline C has all that shortened merely to "*entrance*" (C29).

other aspects of the book's plot or series plotline found in our outline — implies that this was part of the earliest plotline she had in mind for the seven books.

With that said, let's look at what part of the plot each "*Dumbledore*" represents. I will analyze the "*Dumbledore*"s in reverse order.[8]

The second "*Dumbledore*" appears under the first outline (A30) in the context of the Ministry Battle. It is clearly referring to the moment in the published book where Dumbledore saves Harry from Voldemort by the skin of his teeth. When she wrote just "*Dumbledore*", without elaboration, Rowling certainly has in her mind something epic – i.e., Dumbledore does something awesome here. However, there is likely something else she has in mind as well. It is important to notice that this is the very first time (actually, the only time) in the series that Harry messes up in the conclusion of a book. In all four preceding books, Harry tackles and deals with Voldemort himself. Dumbledore is always completely on the sidelines.[9] He is there merely to be the denouement deliverer, explaining to Harry what really went on during the year (and what happened while Harry was unconscious!). In contrast, *Phoenix* is the very first time where Harry does not do a good job and Dumbledore needs to go save him. This, I speculate, is what J.K. Rowling really had in her mind when she wrote just "*Dumbledore*". It is essential for *Phoenix*'s primary plot for Dumbledore to rescue Harry for the

---

[8] This is because the second "*Dumbledore*" has a clear parallel in the final book, but the first one has no clear parallel, as will be discussed.

[9] In *Stone*, Dumbledore is flying to London. In *Chamber*, Dumbledore is out of school due to Ministry decision. In *Azkaban*, Dumbledore sends the crew back in time while he is distracted by the Ministry. In *Goblet*, Dumbledore is not present at the maze and cemetery.

first time in all of the books. Furthermore, this part was so set in Rowlings's mind, it needed no more elaboration than the word "*Dumbledore*". Dumbledore must save Harry for a change, and it had always meant to be that way from Rowling's very first plan.

In contrast, the first appearance of "*Dumbledore*" is harder to parse. Here is its context:

> *Chapter 10 – September / October – Blackout*[10].
> *Plot: Weekend – careers pamphlets – starting to get annoyed with Umbridge – Quidditch practice – Umbridge skulking – scar – Dumbledore – Snape lessons set up.* (Outline C10)

These events end up taking place over several chapters in the published book (chs. 13–14, 24, 29), and there is no event with Dumbledore in any of them! There's definitely a possibility that there was a planned Harry-Dumbledore meeting which ended up being erased from the final plot, but I believe that the actual explanation is something else — "*Dumbledore*" here refers to a part of the plot that is never clearly mentioned in the outline but lingers underfoot, the subplot that I like to call the Dumbledore subplot: that of Dumbledore refusing to look or talk to Harry, giving him the silent treatment. In the books:

> *"Harry, I think you ought to tell Dumbledore your scar hurt."*

---

[10] "*Blackout*" was the working chapter title. It is presumably referring to Harry blacking out due to his scar.

> *It was the second time in two days he had been advised to go to Dumbledore and his answer to Hermione was just the same as his answer to Ron.*
>
> *"I'm not bothering him with this. Like you just said, it's not a big deal. It's been hurting on and off all summer — it was just a bit worse tonight, that's all —"*
>
> *"Harry, I'm sure Dumbledore would want to be bothered by this —"*
>
> *"Yeah," said Harry, before he could stop himself, "that's the only bit of me Dumbledore cares about, isn't it, my scar?"* (*Phoenix* ch. 13)

This[11] is probably the "*Dumbledore*" reference in the draft, which is why it is preceded by the word "*scar*". J.K. Rowling is referring here to Harry refusing to talk to Dumbledore about his scar, which in turn ends up leading to Occlumency lessons. This plot element too was set strongly in Rowling's head; thus, the reference is limited to just "*Dumbledore*". Hence this too must be an important element of *Phoenix*'s plot, and also likely a plot element that was there before the outline was written and hence possibly part of Rowling's very first drafts.

From this flimsy evidence we go "*journeying together through the murky marshes*" of drafts and outlines "*into thickets of wildest guesswork*" (*Prince* ch. 10). What do these two totally disparate plot elements have in common? Furthermore, if we are correct, why were these plot elements so important to Rowling in her original plan? Answering these questions will answer our original question — what was Rowling's intention for the primary plot of *Phoenix* and its place in the plotline for all seven books. I would like to suggest that the primary purpose of *Order*

[11] And the similar conversations with Ron earlier in the chapter.

of the Phoenix from Rowling's very first draft is twofold: First, to set up Harry's loss of trust in Dumbledore, and second: set up the reader's (who views events through Harry's eyes) loss of trust as well.

As John Granger points out (*Beyond Belief*), Harry is generally a stand-in for a Christlike figure, while Dumbledore is a stand-in for God. In the first three books, Dumbledore generally has Godlike powers: He is able to turn himself invisible at will, capable of any and all magic (possibly excluding evil), and rightfully deserves the label of "the most powerful wizard in the world".[12] But more importantly for Granger's point, Dumbledore seems to have Godlike omniscience — seemingly knowing things only a God could have. He magically realizes that Harry has gone after Quirrell: "*Dumbledore when we met him in the Entrance Hall — he already knew — he just said, 'Harry's gone after him, hasn't he?'*" (*Stone* ch. 17). He realizes the Chamber of Secrets is open again and somehow deduces that Lucius Malfoy gave Ginny the diary. And of course, Dumbledore's Godlike knowledge reaches his apex in the climax of *Azkaban*, where he somehow conducts a time travel rescue mission so convoluted that it seems almost impossible for Dumbledore to have coordinated outside being a God: "*'Macnair, if Buckbeak has indeed been stolen, do you really think the thief will have led him away on foot?' said Dumbledore, still sounding amused*" (*Azkaban* ch. 21). This implies knowledge that Dumbledore cannot possibly have had yet: that Harry and Hermione had gone back in time and moved Buckbeak to the

[12] This point is rubbed in as Dumbledore is dubbed "*the only wizard Voldemort ever feared*" (*Goblet* ch. 35, *Phoenix* ch. 36).

forest! He also figures out that Sirius is innocent without having seen any of the evidence that Harry and his friends saw.[13]

All this is necessary for what I propose was a part of J.K. Rowling's original scribbled first draft. She wanted Harry to have complete faith in Dumbledore/God, then doubt him to the depth of his soul, and finally choose to trust him wholeheartedly so that he can rise again as a Christlike figure in complete faith. For that to happen, Rowling has to first build up Dumbledore as an essentially omniscient figure, which she does successfully through the third book.

In the fourth book, however, Rowling starts poking small holes in the Dumbledore-is-omniscient belief. Being the center of the carefully constructed chiasmus the books are,[14] the fourth book manages a wonderful balancing act of making the reader and Harry believe Dumbledore's omniscience while the careful observer will start noticing some shadows in the foe-glass. Primarily, Dumbledore completely misses his best friend being replaced by a Polyjuice-drinker for a full year — right under his nose! That certainly wipes away a large part of the veneer of omniscience from Dumbledore. Yet Harry — and the reader — walk away at the end of *Goblet* impressed by Dumbledore's apparent brilliance and supreme knowledge, because he figured it out! (And at the end of the book too, where Dumbledore is supposed to be figuring things out. Right on schedule!)

It is my contention that the primary plot and purpose of *Phoenix* was precisely this: To finally and totally destroy Harry's — and the reader's — blind trust in Dumbledore. Let us examine

---

[13] For a possible explanation that does not give Dumbledore omniscience, see Khaytman.

[14] For a good discussion of chiasmus in Harry Potter, see Granger, *Harry Potter as Ring Composition and Ring Cycle.*

how Rowling accomplishes this: In the start of *Phoenix*, Dumbledore ignores Harry and gives him the silent treatment. He then orders Harry to attend private lessons with Snape (which the reader knows will be disastrous). At each injustice, Harry's anger grows more and more. But while Harry seethes, we readers nod wisely alongside Ron and Hermione and say, "it's Dumbledore, of course he has a deeper plan!". It is this attitude that Rowling most aspires to break.

She successfully does this in two ways. First, she intentionally has Dumbledore save Harry at the end. This humiliates Harry, who as a teenage boy does not want to be saved by others. But it also humiliates the reader as well. We are used to getting our Harry-performing-awesomeness fix at the end of each book and are looking forward to getting it here. And at the start of *Phoenix*'s climax, it seems we'll get our fair share of it, with our flying Thestrals and cool ministry phone booths. And we know deep down as readers that although Harry messes up, he always does some brave thing and fixes it (sort of like Curious George). When Harry does not actually do anything of significance except for getting Sirius killed, and ends up needing to be saved by Dumbledore, this incites us. What was the whole effort for? We get angry. But Rowling is just getting started.

If you look at the end of the outline, you will notice the text originally read "*explanations from Dumbledore*" (A31). But Rowling has crossed out the word "*explanations*" and instead added "*fall out*". And that is precisely what we are going to get.

When Dumbledore returns with Harry at the denouement of *Phoenix*, Harry is furious and humiliated. His rescue plan has gone amok, and his godfather is dead. But while Harry is certainly angry, we readers are expectant. Surely Dumbledore has some good explanations for what has happened throughout this book. We are still willing to give him the benefit of the doubt. But when Dumbledore lets us down — the whole shebang was just to protect an irrelevant useless prophecy — it is we readers who get mad! We rage and seethe at the pointlessness of the plot and the book! And that is precisely the point! We need to lose our trust in Dumbledore as well, and if Dumbledore had a good explanation, we would not!

And Rowling is not done with us readers (or Harry) yet. Rowling rubs it in, with Dumbledore saying, "*Yet there was a flaw in this wonderful plan of mine ... I cared ... too much!*" (*Phoenix* ch. 37). Harry must have certainly felt upset about that, as he had been ignored by this supposedly caring person the whole year — but it is we readers who are left seething. With our third-party omniscience we now know that Dumbledore apparently did not care at all! He could have kept Harry safe by simply telling him "Hey, if you see a hall of prophecies, don't go there". He could have done something more useful throughout the year — pretty much anything — than entirely ignore Harry. He could have used his godlike omniscience to make sure Harry was left unharmed by Umbridge. Yet he does nothing at all. Rowling does this purposely to ensure that it is not just Harry who now mistrusts Dumbledore but also us as well.

This may also be the reason why Rowling switched the roles of Dumbledore's Army and the Order of the Phoenix from the outline to the published book. (In the outline, the Order of the Phoenix refers to Harry's secret Defence Against the Dark Arts classes, while Dumbledore's Army refers to the group who battled Voldemort in the first war, the reverse of the published book). Dumbledore's betrayal of Harry's trust is much more of a gut punch to the reader once they see that Harry named his personal class after him. That gutpunch just isn't there if Harry's class was named the Order of the Phoenix.[15]

All of this sets us up wonderfully for the sixth book, where Dumbledore's death needs to be seen as a possible mistake of Dumbledore's for the series plotline to work. This would be impossible should Dumbledore still seem omniscient to the reader.

Finally, this sets us up for Harry finally regaining trust in Dumbledore in the seventh book, in the passage I find most touching, almost sacrosanct, of all seven books:

> *Harry knew what he had seen. A piercing blue eye had looked out of the mirror fragment, and then help had come. Help will always be given at Hogwarts to those who ask for it.*
>
> *...Harry understood, and yet did not understand. His instinct was telling him one thing, his brain quite another. The Dumbledore in Harry's head smiled, surveying Harry over the tips of his fingers, pressed together as if in prayer.*
>
> *You gave Ron the Deluminator. You understood him ... you gave him a way back ...*
>
> *And you understood Wormtail too. ... You knew there was a bit of regret there, somewhere. ...*
>
> *And if you knew them ... what did you know about me, Dumbledore?*
>
> *Am I meant to know, but not to seek? Did you know how hard I'd feel that? Is that why you made it this*

[15] For more on this role switch, see the essay by Beatrice Groves in this volume.

> *difficult? So I'd have time to work that out?* (*Hallows* ch. 24)

In this passage, Harry, and the reader, regain their trust in Dumbledore, concluding what I believe was one of Rowling's original plotlines on her first draft all those years ago.

In conclusion, *Phoenix*'s plot seems useless, both in the book itself and especially in the seven-book plotline. However, based on the *Phoenix* outline, we can perhaps find a possible reason why this is. Rowling describes the Dumbledore plotlines in two places simply as "*Dumbledore*". Based on what we know from lexicographers and Jewish law scholars, when something appears without explanation it is usually because that element was already set in the writer's mind. Thus, one can conclude that the Dumbledore plotline was one of the story's original plot elements. If that is true, it explains the original point of *Phoenix*: The purpose is for Harry and the reader to lose trust in Dumbledore, setting the stage for the sixth and seventh books where lack of trust in Dumbledore is required for the series plotline to work.

Works Cited

Anelli, Melissa. *Harry, a History*. Simon & Schuster, 2008.

Brody, Robert. *Mishna and Tosefta Studies*. Magnus Press, 2015.

DarklzBlo. "What's your least favorite Harry Potter book from all 7 books?" *Reddit*, 30 Nov. 2023.

Granger, John. Guest. "Harry Potter." *Beyond Belief*. BBC Radio 4, 23 Aug. 2021.

———. *Harry Potter as Ring Composition and Ring Cycle*. Lulu, 2010.

Khaytman, Irvin. *Dumbledore*. Media Lab Books, 2021.

Roonil_Wazlib97. Comment on "In OOTP, Why It's So Important for Order to Prevent Voldemort from Getting the Prophecy?" by EitherPhase5676. *Reddit*, 28 Feb. 2023.

Rowling, J.K. "My Story." *J.K. Rowling's Stories*, 9 Sept. 2021.

Singer, Natasha. "Scouring the Web to Make New Words 'Lookupable.'" *The New York Times*, 4 Oct. 2015, sec. BU, p. 3.

Spartz, Emerson, and Ben Schoen. *Harry Potter Should Have Died: Controversial Views from the #1 Fan Site*. Ulysses Press, 2009.

Spartz, Emerson, et al. *Mugglenet's What Will Happen in Harry Potter 7: Who Lives, Who Dies, Who Falls in Love, and How Will the Adventure Finally End*. Ulysses Press, 2006.

Stamper, Kory. *Word by Word*. Vintage, 2017.

Taub, Moshe. *Jews in the New World: History, Halachah, and Hashkafa*. Mosaica Press, 2024.

BEATRICE GROVES

The Phoenix and the Flame

THE SYMBOLIC NAME CHANGE OF *THE ORDER OF THE PHOENIX*

Name changes are a significant part of the writing process. As Colin Burrow (17) has argued, "*when we meet a name that just seems right ... a peculiar magic happens that is related to aesthetic pleasure: the instance both modifies and validates the invisible conventions that we didn't know we knew.*" Dickens, for example, ruminated on his names for some time – the eponymous hero of *Martin Chuzzlewit* was variously dubbed Sweezleden, Sweezleback, Sweezlewag, Chuzzltoe, Chuzzle-boy, Chubblewig, and Chuzzlewig before Dickens hit on the name by which he is now known. Some of J.K. Rowling's characters have gone through Dickensian-sounding name changes (such as Hedwig, who was originally Kallicrates and then Widdicombe[1]) and these discarded names may lurk for decades in her head. A name she did not end up using for a Defence Against the Dark Arts teacher, for example (who appeared in her first notes as "*Oakden Hernshaw*" or "*Oakden Hobday*" [Lists of Hogwarts subjects and teachers]) reappears nearly thirty years later as Carl Oakden in *Troubled Blood*. Rowling has noted how fundamental the correct naming, and hence name changes, are to her writing process: "*names are really crucial to me, and some of my characters have had eight or nine names before I hit the right one. And for some reason I just can't move on until I know I've called them the right thing – that's very fundamental to me*" (*The Connection*).

In *The Order of the Phoenix* outline there is one example of a change in the designation of a character which is not a name change, as such, but which likewise illuminates the author's writing process. Rowling does not change the name of James Potter when she gives Occlumency lessons the heading "*Snape/Harry/Father*," but calling James "*Father*," (or, in one heading, "*Dad*") while Snape and Harry are both given their names, means that James is referred to only through his relation to Harry. This is something that Shakespeare also did in his first drafts, indicating the way in which minor characters are perceived by the author in relation to the main characters. We have no such treasure trove for Shakespeare's craft as a handwritten outline, but early printings of his plays have been scoured by critics for evidence of anomalies in the underlying manuscripts which might provide clues for some of Shakespeare's own first thoughts. In the case of the second

---

[1] This can be seen on Rowling's first draft of *Philosopher's Stone* Chapter 6, where she crosses out "*Kallicrates*" as the name Harry originally gives his owl, and replaces it with "*Widdicombe*", before deciding on the final name, "*Hedwig*".

printing of *Romeo and Juliet – The Most Excellent and lamentable Tragedie, of Romeo and Iuliet*, printed in 1599 – this can be seen by the variable speech prefixes of Juliet's mother Lady Capulet. In the Folio she is designated as "Lady Capulet" throughout, but in the second quarto she is "*Old La[dy]*" and "*Mo[ther]*" (sig. B4v–Cr). These unstable speech prefixes appear to record Shakespeare's own creative process in thinking of Lady Capulet in relation to Juliet, just as Rowling's "*Father*" and "*Dad*" indicates that she is thinking about James through the lens of his relation to Harry.[2]

The most significant name change between the planned outline for *Order of the Phoenix* and the published novel is, however, that the name "*Order of the Phoenix*" originally belonged to the teenage resistance group (Harry's league against Umbridge) while the adult group was known as "*Dumbledore's Army.*" Each of these aspects of the plot are given their own column (with the headings "*DA*" and "*O of P*"/ "*OP*") and the "*DA*" column stipulates that at 12 Grimmauld Place, Dumbledore's Army "*Meet for first time*" (C4). Conversely, in the "OP" column the first entry occurs much later in the novel, when the "*Idea for Order of the Phoenix*" first arises (C12). This swapping of the designation of the teenaged and adult groups is particularly striking because Rowling has dated her work on the outline to 2001–2002, thus placing it after the unveiling of the book's title in 2000.[3] If this dating is correct, it means that the

---

[2] Further exploration of changes seen in the outline's characters can be found in Alice's essay earlier in this volume.

[3] In the *History of Magic* exhibition, this outline was displayed with wall text attributing a 2017 quote to Rowling, stating that "*these plans date from around 2001/2.*" In October 2000, Rowling announced that the title was going to be *Harry Potter and the Order of the Phoenix* (Today Show).

novel was originally named after Harry's group, not Dumbledore's league against Voldemort.

In the published novel it is clear that the two organizations are mirror-images of each-other – the Hogwarts' students (like their adult counterparts) band together to resist evil using the interconnected strengths of skill in Defence against the Dark Arts and the power of friendship. And while in the *Order of the Phoenix* itself the adults are far more effective than the students in resisting Voldemort, it is the teenagers who will be crucial in Voldemort's ultimate defeat. In the Battle of Hogwarts, the adults do sterling work defending the castle, but – in one of my favorite moments of the series – it is the erstwhile members of the teenaged group who appear at the critical moment (as the adults did in the Battle at the Ministry). Luna, Ernie and Seamus appear with the Patronuses Harry had taught them to conjure in the Room of Requirement and save the day when all seemed lost: "*'We're all still here,' [Luna] whispered, 'we're still fighting'*" (*Hallows* ch. 32).

Re-Ordering Dumbledore's Army

The switching of the monikers *Dumbledore's Army* and the *Order of the Phoenix* between the manuscript outline and the printed novel highlights the parallels between the two groups, but it also draws attention to precisely how interchangeable these names are. Both *Army* and *Order* are names for official, adult organizations: *Order* is a name taken from the British honors' system (the "Order of Merlin" is named after the oldest and most senior chivalric Order in the British Isles: The Order of the Garter [Groves, *Literary Allusion* 42–3]). Both *Army* and *Order* are high status words which can only be used by a group of teenagers disobeying their teachers in a slightly tongue-in-cheek manner. Likewise, the other half of the name – *Dumbledore* or *Phoenix* – draws attention to the deep connection between Dumbledore and Fawkes. Fawkes is no mere pet, and Dumbledore's phoenix Patronus symbolizes a fundamental part of himself.[4] Throughout the novels Dumbledore and Fawkes are closely aligned – envisaged almost as aspects of each other. When Harry hears phoenix song he thinks of Dumbledore: "*[Harry] felt as though the song was inside him instead of just around him ... it was the sound he connected with Dumbledore, and it was almost as though a friend was speaking in his ear*" (*Goblet* ch. 34). Conversely, the sight of Dumbledore sustains him like phoenix song: "*A powerful emotion had risen in Harry's chest at the sight of Dumbledore, a fortified, hopeful feeling rather like that which phoenix song gave him*" (*Phoenix* ch. 8). It is almost as though Dumbledore is phoenix song made visible and phoenix song is Dumbledore rendered as music: they are different expressions of the same hope-filled and sustaining thing.[5]

It makes sense, therefore, that the names *Dumbledore's Army* and *The Order of the Phoenix* should likewise be interchangeable for Rowling. Their being so expresses something symbolically important about the alignment of Dumbledore and the Phoenix

---

[4] In *Crimes of Grindelwald* and *The Secrets of Dumbledore* the phoenix becomes a Dumbledore family emblem (see also Groves, "The Phoenix and the Qilin").

[5] Dumbledore's own musicality is only mentioned in the opening novel of the series, but it is clearly a major part of Rowling's understanding of his character: "*'Ah, music,' he said, wiping his eyes. 'A magic beyond all we do here!'*" (*Stone* ch. 7). Dumbledore's Chocolate Frog Card notes that he enjoys chamber music (*Stone* ch. 6), and he is named after a bumblebee "*because he is a musical person. And I imagine him humming to himself all the time*" (*Larry King Live*).

– and the connection of both with Harry. One of the resistance groups is named after Fawkes, one is led by Harry, and both are led by or named after Dumbledore. Harry, Fawkes, and Dumbledore are the three who unite as a figurehead for those resisting the Dark Lord.

Fawkes and the Holy Spirit

A number of critics, such as John Granger and Connie Neal, have shown that the Christian framework is more germane to *Harry Potter* than we might initially expect.[6] As Rowling herself has said (referencing Neal's work[7]): "*there was a Christian commentator who said that Harry Potter had been the Christian church's biggest missed opportunity. And I thought, there's someone who actually has their eyes open*" (*The Student*). There are evident parallels throughout the novels between Dumbledore – with his paternal guidance and benign omniscience – and God the Father. Even more clearly, aspects of Harry's journey – from his three-day unconsciousness after facing Voldemort in *Philosopher's Stone* to his final rising from the dead – recall Christ's story. It has been openly acknowledged by Rowling that Harry "*does have certain messiah traits. I chose that on purpose*" (*de Volkskrant*). This is signaled throughout the novels, but it is especially visible in *Deathly Hallows* with the Christmas visit to Harry's birthplace, the *Via Dolorosa* of Harry's walk towards death, the *Pièta* of his "dead" body carried by Hagrid and the breaking down of barriers between Hogwarts's Houses after Harry's return from the dead

---

[6] Granger, *Deathly Hallow Lectures*; Neal, *The Gospel According to Harry Potter*; see also Groves, *Literary Allusion*.

[7] For the identification of Neal, see Granger, "The Adeel Amini – Jo Rowling Interview."

as "*their leader and symbol, their saviour and their guide*" (ch. 36; see also Groves, *Literary Allusion*, 58–90). The strongest early hints of these "messiah traits," however, occur in *Order of the Phoenix* with the explicit acknowledgement of Harry's "*saving-people thing*" (ch. 32) and in the revelation that Voldemort, Herod-like, tried to kill Harry as baby because of a prophecy about his future power (see Groves, *Literary Allusion*, 86–90). Given Harry's "messiah traits" and Dumbledore's all-knowing fatherhood, it makes symbolic sense that Fawkes, and especially his song (the invisible, powerful and sustaining expression of his nature) should be aligned in with the Holy Spirit.

Fawkes's name, recognisable to English readers as a pun on Guy Fawkes, is a comic nod to his status as a firebird. Rowling has spoken of the firebird as an archetype that reaches across cultures expressing something innate to the human mind:

> *I am even more fascinated by the fact that discrete cultures who'd never met create such similar archetypes and such similar creatures. So, we see the "firebird" – the phoenix as I called it – but you see the creation of a firebird throughout different cultures. And what is that telling us about what it is to be human and what lives at the back of our minds, in our subconscious?* (*Fantastic Beasts: A Natural History*)

In the bible the Holy Spirit is figured both as fire ("*cloven tongues like as of fire*" [*King James Version*, Acts 2.3][8]) and a bird: "*the Spirit of God descending like a dove*" (Matt. 3.16). The

---

[8] All biblical references are from the King James Bible (1611), as this is the translation used in the biblical quotations within *Harry Potter*.

fiery tongues of the Holy Spirit that light on the heads of the disciples at Pentecost do not burn them, just as the burning bush from which God speaks in Exodus burns but "*was not consumed*" (Exod. 3.2). The phoenix firebird, likewise, is unharmed by the flames that consume him – born again to new life through each burning.

The *Order of the Phoenix* outline illuminates a way in which Fawkes's role has been extended in the published novel – and it is one which extenuates his fiery, saving power. In *Order of the Phoenix*, Dumbledore, threatened with prosecution, expresses his effortless superiority by escaping with Fawkes in "*a flash of fire*" (eliciting one of the best lines of the book from Phineas Nigellus: "*You know, Minister, I disagree with Dumbledore on many counts ... but you cannot deny he's got style ...*" [ch. 27]). Fawkes' role in Dumbledore's escape here is absent from the draft in which Dumbledore is taken to Azkaban (B23; C23), which means that Fawkes's importance has been increased in the finished novel: "*Fawkes circled the office and swooped low over him. Dumbledore released Harry, raised his hand and grasped the phoenix's long golden tail. There was a flash of fire and the pair of them were gone*" (*Phoenix* ch. 27).

This escape via Fawkes's golden tail feathers is important, in part, because it echoes Harry's Fawkes-enabled escape in *Chamber of Secrets*. That appearance of Fawkes, predicated as it was on Harry's declaration of his faith in his Headmaster, is the most important symbolic moment in the series embodying the relationship between Dumbledore and his phoenix.[9] Both Fawkes's innate connection with Dumbledore and his saving power is stressed in these paired scenes. As Dumbledore tells

[9] For more on the Christian symbolism of this scene, see Groves, *Literary Allusion*, 60–80.

Harry in *Chamber of Secrets*, "*you must have shown me real loyalty down in the Chamber. Nothing but that could have called Fawkes to you*" (ch. 18). In the Bible it is noted that the Holy Spirit is sent to those who trust in God: "*Trust in the Lord with all thine heart ... and he shall direct thy paths*" (Prov. 3.5–6).

The Holy Spirit gives distinct spiritual gifts to each of the faithful (1 Cor. 12) and Fawkes, likewise, brings Harry the gift of the Sorting Hat (*Chamber* ch. 17), which functions in many ways like a spiritual gift, as it is only due to Harry's own purity of heart that he can draw from it the saving sword. In the series as a whole Fawkes also gives Harry one of his tail feathers as the core of his wand (*Goblet* ch. 36) – a gift that likewise has a spiritual dimension for, as we know, "*the wand chooses the wizard*" (*Stone* ch. 5). Feathers symbolize flight (the reason the Holy Spirit, which "*bloweth where it listeth*" [John 3.8] is symbolized by birds), so it is fitting that Fawkes's feathers play such a providential role in the story: both creating the saving core of Harry's wand and transporting Harry, Dumbledore, Ron, Ginny, (and even Lockhart) to safety. (It is tempting to note that the physical escape that Fawkes enables with his strong tail feathers links with a surprising action of the Holy Spirit when it physically transports Philip in Acts [8:39–40]). Harry's trust in Dumbledore calls Fawkes to him, and Fawkes brings to Harry gifts which will enable him to defeat the Dark Lord and then carries him to freedom, creating a strong echo of the providential action of the Holy Spirit, as promised in the Pentecostal fulfillment of the prophecy in Joel "*And it shall come to pass, that whosoever shall call on the name of the Lord shall be saved*" (Acts 2.21).

Harry's tail-feather wand also means, in a sense, that Fawkes is with him always. This phoenix feather wand saves Harry at the end of *Goblet of Fire* (ch. 36) and again at the opening of

Deathly Hallows "*the noble phoenix feather wand had saved him*" (ch. 34). It also aligns with Harry's faith in Dumbledore as, just as Fawkes is sent to Harry in *Chamber* when he expresses his belief in Dumbledore (ch. 17), so it is only when Harry's phoenix feather wand is broken that he reaches his nadir of doubt:

> *And his fury at Dumbledore broke over him now like lava, scorching him inside, wiping out every other feeling. Out of sheer desperation they had talked themselves into believing that Godric's Hollow held answers, and convinced themselves that they were supposed to go back, that it was all part of some secret path laid out for them by Dumbledore; but there was no map, no plan. Dumbledore had left them to grope in the darkness, to wrestle with unknown and undreamed of terrors alone and unaided: nothing was explained, nothing was given freely, they had no sword, and now, Harry had no wand.* (*Hallows* ch. 18)

Shakespeare's Phoenix

Shakespeare is one of Rowling's favorite authors and just as I began this essay with a link between Rowling and Shakespeare's creative processes, I've written extensively elsewhere about his influence on her writing.[10] A further link is the possible influence of Shakespeare's poem *The Phoenix and Turtle* on Rowling's use of a phoenix as a wider Trinitarian symbol (rather than just using its traditional Christic

[10] See Groves, *Literary Allusion* 23–24, 81–97. See also Groves's "Shakespeare and Harry Potter," "A Shakespearean Source," "Hits-and-Misses," and "It's Just Like Waking Up."

symbolism). Shakespeare's "*sublime and mysterious*" (Beauregard 131) poem is a threnody – a mourning song – for a phoenix and a turtle dove. It has been argued since at least the 1950s that the poem's opacity relates to its poetic evocation of the Trinity: "*The Phoenix and Turtle are distinct persons, yet one in love, on the analogy of the Father and the Son in the Holy Ghost*" (Cunningham 276). The two-in-oneness of the beloved pair is expressed as a numerical mystery modeled on the three-in-oneness of the Trinity:

> *So they loved as love in twain,*
> *Had the essence but in one,*
> *Two distincts, division none:*
> *Number there in love was slain.* (*PhT* 25–28)

This language of "essence," "division," and "distincts" is explicitly Trinitarian, used by contemporary theologians drawing on the work of Thomas Aquinas who, as Colin Burrow notes, argued that while "division" (*divisio*) must not be used to describe the persons of the Trinity, "distinction" (*distinctio*) could be: "*Two distincts, division none*" (Shakespeare, *The Complete Sonnets*, notes to lines 26–27). As J. V. Cunningham noted in 1952, "*the relation of lover and beloved in Shakespeare's poem is that of the Persons of the Trinity, and the technical language employed is that of scholastic discussion on the subject*" (Cunningham 273). Walter Cohen in *The Norton Shakespeare* (just such a one-volume Shakespeare as Rowling has spoken of taking with her to a desert island [*New York Times*]) echoes this argument, writing that "*behind the emphasis on the paradoxical unity of two separate beings lies the mystery of the Christian Trinity as understood in Scholastic theology*" (Cohen 1973). Cohen's explanatory essay in *The Norton Shakespeare* made this reading available to a wider audience and it seems possible that *Harry Potter*'s evocation of the Phoenix as part of Trinitarian (rather than simply Christic) imagery, could have been inspired by Shakespeare's own numinous phoenix-symbolism.

Phoenix Song

As Rowling wrote in *Fantastic Beasts and Where to Find Them*, the textbook she published while working on this plot-outline for *Order of the Phoenix*, "*Phoenix song is magical: it is reputed to increase the courage of the pure of heart and to strike fear into the hearts of the impure.*" (*Beasts*) When Dumbledore leaves Hogwarts he makes a numinous promise – "*help will always be given at Hogwarts to those who ask for it*" (*Chamber* ch. 14, 15) – which resonates with a promise given by Christ: "*Ask, and it shall be given you*" (Matt. 7.7). When Harry asks for help when he is trapped down in the Chamber of Secrets, it is given to him via the medium of Fawkes. Along with the literal gifts of the Sorting Hat and Riddle's diary, Fawkes also brings Harry the spiritual gift of courage via his song: "*eerie, spine-tingling, unearthly; it lifted the hair on Harry's scalp and made his heart feel as though it was swelling to twice its normal size*" (*Chamber* ch. 17). This heart-swelling courage comes from the confidence that he is no longer alone: "*he might not see what use Fawkes or the Sorting Hat were, but he was no longer alone, and he waited with mounting courage for Riddle to stop laughing*" (*Chamber* ch. 17).

When Christ leaves his followers he promises, in a section of the gospels traditionally known as the farewell discourse (John 14–17), that they will be sent "*the Comforter, which is the Holy Ghost, whom the Father will send in my name*" (John 14.26).

Fawkes is likewise sent to Harry as a comforter, not only in the Chamber of Secrets but also in the time of his greatest sorrow:

> *Somewhere out in the darkness, a phoenix was singing in a way Harry had never heard before: a stricken lament of terrible beauty. And Harry felt, as he had felt about phoenix song before, that the music was inside him, not without: it was his own grief turned magically to song that echoed across the grounds and through the castle windows.*
>
> *How long they all stood there, listening, he did not know, nor why it seemed to ease their pain a little to listen to the sound of their mourning.* (*Prince* ch. 29)

Jesus promises that "*the Comforter whom the Father will send will bring all things to your remembrance, whatsoever I have said unto you*" (John 14.26). And, after Fawkes finishes singing, Harry does indeed remember – and is comforted by – a saying of Dumbledore: "*'He will only be gone from the school when none here are loyal to him,' said Harry, smiling in spite of himself*" (*Prince* ch. 30).

Fawkes's song weaves through the whole of chapter 29 ("The Phoenix Lament") dipping in and out of the reader's consciousness, but always present and when Harry listens to it, it brings him comfort. Fawkes sings a threnody – a lament or mourning song like Shakespeare's *Phoenix and the Turtle* – beautifully expressed as Harry's "*own grief turned magically to song.*" By expressing the healing of this song as transfigured grief this moment also reveals it, like the Holy Spirit, to be love: "*Grief, it seemed, drove Voldemort out … though Dumbledore, of course, would have said that it was love*" (*Hallows* ch. 24).

The comfort that Fawkes brings Harry is clearest in the paired books of *Chamber* and *Half-Blood Prince*, but it forms an important background to *Order of the Phoenix* too.[11] This is the book in which Harry ceases to believe that Dumbledore is always on his side and starts to lose his faith in his Headmaster and yet Dumbledore is always working for his good. The title is a reminder of this – of Dumbledore's continuous action even when he seems to be absent, acting through those who act in his name. The name *The Order of the Phoenix* is one of the clearest Holy Spirit parallels in the series, as it underlines how the friends who band together to fight evil are inspired and nurtured by the Phoenix. The name-swap between the outline and the published novel means that both the secret groups who meet together to secretly resist the Dark Lord – organizations that sound like Wizarding World parallels to the persecuted early church – are called the *Order of the Phoenix*. These groups are symbolically sustained by Fawkes just as the Church is inspired and sustained by the Holy Spirit.

One connection illustrative of this idea, which is present in the outline (but lacking in the finished novel), is that an important "Order of the Phoenix" event occurs at Easter. Chapter 23 has in its "*Plot*" column: "*Easter – discovery of the Order of the Phoenix*" (B23; C23). This revelation of the group at Easter fits with its religious resonances (as does Harry's profound return to faith in Dumbledore as he digs Dobby's grave in the Easter holidays in *Deathly Hallows*). Easter is likewise important in the published *Order of the Phoenix*, creating a strong moment of food-fellowship between Harry

[11] For the chiastic structuring of the series, in which the first and last, second and sixth, third and fifth books are paired, see Groves, *Literary Allusion*, 8–10, 139–44.

and Ginny as they share Easter chocolate and Harry opens up to her. In the outline the Easter-theme is even clearer as it was at Easter that Dumbledore sacrificially took the blame for Harry's act of resistance.

Conclusion

The naming of the fifth novel of the series *The Order of the Phoenix* draws attention to one of *Harry Potter*'s most important symbolic animals. The plot-outline of *Order of the Phoenix* intimately connects "Dumbledore's Army" and "Order of the Phoenix" by revealing that Rowling exchanged their names. It is a name-change that reveals the interconnectedness of Dumbledore and Fawkes, suggesting a deeper symbolic bond between them than has generally been realized, and supporting a reading of Fawkes in which his actions carry a Trinitarian resonance.

The phoenix is a firebird, which fits with the fiery sending of the Holy Spirit at Pentecost and there is also another moment in *Order of the Phoenix* which contains a parodic memory of the first Pentecost. Peeves teases Harry with the idea that he is going mad: "'*What is it this time, my fine Potty friend? Hearing voices? Seeing visions? Speaking in –' Peeves blew a gigantic raspberry '— tongues?*'" (*Phoenix* ch. 12). Hearing voices and seeing visions are not only accurate descriptions of what has been happening to Harry but are also quintessential aspects of religious experience in the bible (from the calling of Samuel to the vision on the road to Damascus). "*Speaking in tongues,*" however, points specifically to Pentecost, because the phrase derives directly from the experience of the disciples at Pentecost: "*and they were all filled with the Holy Ghost, and began to speak with other tongues, as the Spirit gave them utterance*"

(Acts 2.4). This first Pentecost also imparts a miraculous ability, like Harry's ability to understand Parseltongue, to interpret languages: "*every man heard them speak in his own language*" (Acts 2.6). Simultaneously, it recalls a prophecy about seeing visions, as Peter describes Pentecost as the fulfillment of Joel's prophecy: "*I will pour out of my Spirit upon all flesh... and your young men shall see visions*" (Acts 2.17). Peeves' mocking of Harry "*hearing voices*" and "*seeing visions,*" therefore forms a subtle echo of the young men who "*shall see visions*" and those who "*heard them speak in his own language*" at Pentecost.

It is a subtle echo, however, which is rendered into an explicit allusion only when Peeves likewise accuses Harry of "*Speaking in... tongues.*" This pun on Harry's ability to speak Parseltongue directly echoes the most famous miracle of Pentecost: "*they were all filled with the Holy Ghost, and began to speak with other tongues*" (Acts 2.4). It seems deeply in keeping with the symbolism for which this chapter has been arguing that one of *Harry Potter*'s most extensive biblical echoes should be about the sending of the Holy Spirit. And that it should occur in the book which is named after Fawkes: *The Order of the Phoenix*.

Works Cited

Beauregard, David. "'The Mutual Flame of Love': Spiritual Marriage in Shakespeare's *The Phoenix and Turtle*." *Religion and the Arts*, vol. 15, 2011, pp. 131–47.

The Bible. King James Version, 1611.

Burrow, Colin. "I, Lowborn Cur" Review of *Literary Names: Personal Names in English Literature*, by Alastair Fowler. *London Review of Books*, vol. 34 no. 22, 22 November 2012, pp. 15–17.

Cohen, Walter. "The Phoenix and Turtle." *The Norton Shakespeare*, edited by Stephen Greenblatt et al., 3rd ed., W.W. Norton & Co., 2016, pp. 1973–75.

Cunningham, J. V. "'Essence' and the *Phoenix and Turtle.*" *English Literary History*, vol. 4, 1952, pp. 265–76.

Fantastic Beasts: The Crimes of Grindelwald. Directed by David Yates, Warner Brother, 2018.

Fantastic Beasts: The Secrets of Dumbledore. Directed by David Yates, Warner Brothers., 2022.

Granger, John. "The Adeel Amini – Jo Rowling Interview." *Hogwarts Professor*, 30 Mar. 2008. Nota Bene, Feb. 2018.

———. *The Deathly Hallows Lectures: The Hogwarts Professor Explains Harry's Final Adventure.* Zossima Press, 2008.

Groves, Beatrice. "Hits-and-Misses, Folk Horror and Shakespearean Pastoral: Running Grave First Thoughts." *Hogwarts Professor*, 31 Oct. 2023.

———. "'It's Just Like Waking Up, Right?': 'Crimes of Grindelwald', Kipling, and Shakespeare's Midsummer Dreaming." *MuggleNet*, 12 Nov. 2018.

———. *Literary Allusion in Harry Potter*. Routledge, 2017.

———. "The Phoenix and the Qilin in 'Secrets of Dumbledore': Fantastic Bestiaries and Where to Find Them – Part 3." *MuggleNet*, 7 Apr. 2022.

———. "Shakespeare and *Harry Potter* – Part 1." *MuggleNet*, 28 June 2017.

———. "A Shakespearean Source for the Four-Point Character Conflict in *Harry Potter*?" *MuggleNet*, 23 Apr. 2018.

Jones, Valerie. "The Phoenix and the Resurrection." *The Mark of the Beast: The Medieval Bestiary in Art, Life and Literature*, edited by Debra Hassig, Garland Publishing, 1999, pp. 99–116.

Rowling, J.K. "Chapter Six: The Journey from Platform Nine and Three Quarters." Handwritten manuscript draft. British Library, exhibited as part of *Writing Britain: Wastelands to Wonderlands*, 11 May–25 Sept. 2012.

———. Handwritten lists of Hogwarts subjects and teachers. Facsimile. Originally published on *J.K. Rowling Official Site*, 9 Mar. 2006 and 31 Oct. 2007. Later included in *Harry Potter: A History of Magic*, British Library, 2017, pp. 124–25.

———. Interview. "By the Book: J.K. Rowling." *The New York Times*, 14 Oct. 2012, p. BR8. *Sunday Book Review.*

———. Interview by Adeel Amini. *The Student* [Edinburgh], 4 March 2008.

———. Interview by Christopher Lydon. *The Connection.* WBUR, 12 Oct. 1999.

———. Interview by Katie Couric. *Today Show*. NBC, 20 Oct. 2000.

———. Interview by Larry King. "J.K. Rowling Discusses the Surprising Success of 'Harry Potter.'" *Larry King Live*. CNN, 20 Oct. 2000.

———. Interview by Stephen Fry. *Fantastic Beasts: A Natural History. BBC One*, 27 Feb. 2022.

———. Interview by Wilma de Rek. *de Volkskrant*. 17 Nov. 2007. Translated from Dutch: "*Ja, hij heeft messias-trekjes. Daar heb ik bewust voor gekozen*".

———. "*These plans date from around 2001/2.*" Wall text for *Planning the Order of the Phoenix. Harry Potter: A History of Magic*, 20 Oct. 2017–28 Feb. 2018, British Library. *Printed in Harry Potter: A Journey Through a History of Magic*, British Library, 20 Oct. 2017, p. 128.

——— [*published as* Robert Galbraith]. *Troubled Blood*. Sphere, 2020.

Shakespeare, William. "Let the bird of loudest lay" (*The Phoenix and the Turtle*). *The Complete Sonnets and Poems*, edited by Colin Burrow, Oxford University Press, 2002, lines 25–28.

———. *The Most Excellent and Lamentable Tragedie of Romeo and Iuliet. Newly Corrected, Augmented, and Amended.* Cuthbert Burby, 1599. sig. B4v–Cr.

Neal, Connie. *The Gospel According to Harry Potter, Revised and Expanded Edition: The Spiritual Journey of the World's Greatest Seeker*. Westminster/John Knox Press, 2008.

JOHN GRANGER

J.K. Rowling's Phoenix 'Ring Within a Ring'

The structure of Harry's trip through the Department of Mysteries and what it suggests about her planning grids

My task in this anthology is to take a contrarian approach by highlighting an example of the structural artistry in *Phoenix*, none of which is part of Rowling's grids A, B, or C. This makes the point that the much greater effort of her planning that makes the longest *Potter* novel the work of genius that it is, took place well after her first notes on its skeletal plot sequence. The example I will focus on is *Phoenix*'s ring-within-the-ring, the Battle in the Department of Mysteries. Let's talk about the essentials, then, of ring writing.

According to Mary Douglas in her *Thinking in Circles* (35–38), a literary ring has seven distinctive features. I have reduced these to four: (1) a story circle latch of beginning and end, (2) a 'middle' or story-turn that reflect the beginning and the ending, (3) parallels in chiastic sequence between story characters, events, and dialogue between the story going to the middle point and returning to the latch from it, the so-called 'turtle-back' lines, and (4) rings within the story ring. Represented in a diagram it looks like a turtle's back *(see below)*; Rowling's preference is for seven-part rings and, if the *Potter* series is any indication, she may be writing as often as not in an asterisk rather than a traditional ring.

Sample ring composition construction

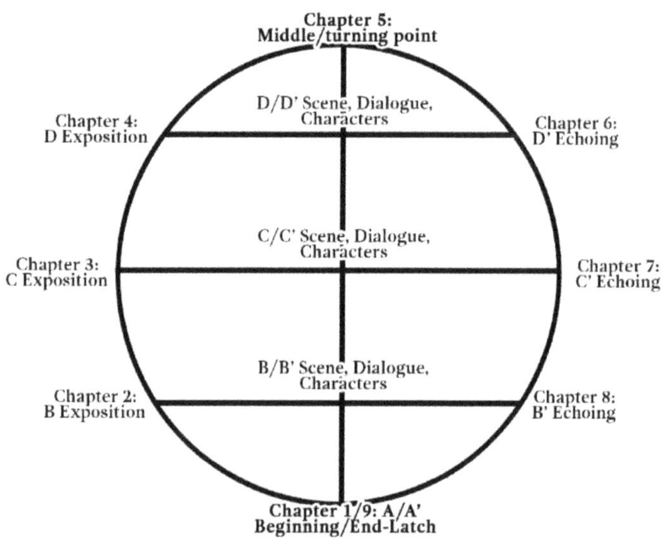

Beginning-Middle-and-End: Echoing with Emphasis at Finale or at Center

In 2010 I gave a talk to *The Group That Shall Not Be Named* in New York City at the Samsung Center which revealed this structural artistry inside the *Potter* novels individually and as a series. I published those lecture notes with attendant graphs and charts as *Harry Potter as Ring Composition and Ring Cycle: The Magical Structure and Transcendent Meaning of the Hogwarts Saga*. Just as that work built on the insights of Joyce Odell and Brett Kendall, so in the intervening years other Potter Pundits, Rowling Readers, and Serious Strikers have documented the parallelism within Rowling's work, within her series, even between her series.[1]

Because the ring structure of *Phoenix* and its place in the seven-part series ring-asterisk has been in print for almost fifteen years and is still available for easy reference elsewhere, I will not review that here. What follows is the internal ring of the Department of Mysteries battle, all explained in terms of latches, turns, and turtle-back parallels per Douglas. It is assumed that any reader of a Rowling Library anthology, especially a collection of essays on Rowling's grid charts, is very, very familiar with the plot points of *The Order of the Phoenix* and would feel insulted by unnecessary explanations of the parallels involved. I have, consequently, stripped this down to the bones.

The several grid charts more or less resemble the final product in story progression. I offer the thesis, however, that in those grids' not reflecting the chiastic parallels of the book that give it its significant subconscious heft, those charts are only the roughest of sketches of the intricate published novel. I also will argue that Rowling's "Department of Mysteries" and Harry and

[1] For a collection of links to that work through the years see Granger, "Ring Composition."

Company's heroic journey through it reveal both the esoteric meaning of the series, love's victory over death, as well as the meaning of ring writing, how the structure itself carries within it the thematic message of the story.

The Ring Within a Ring in *The Order of the Phoenix*: The Importance of the Department of Mysteries Adventure

Before the discussion of the structure of the forty pages in an almost nine-hundred-page work, the obvious needs to be said aloud, namely, *Phoenix* turns on this adventure: almost everything in it before the conflict in the Hall of Prophecy points to it and everything after reflects it. Harry "visits" the Department of Mysteries repeatedly in his day and night dreams throughout the book and the grid charts make clear this structure; Rowling dedicates a column in every stage of her several charts to these Voldemort induced dreams. In the Hall, Harry gains possession of a physical object that contains the underlying narrative of his entire life, namely, the Prophecy, the revelation of which and Harry's coming to understand himself in light of it in Dumbledore's office (and the two subsequent novels in the series!) uncover at last what has been driving the Dark Lord from the inciting incident of his attack on the Potter family so many years ago.

If this revelation of the story-behind-the-story were not enough, the forty-page journey through the Department of Mysteries climaxes with the death of Sirius Black, Harry's Godfather and last connection with his parents, and acts as prelude to the duel between Voldemort and Dumbledore in the Ministry Entry Hall. That duel ends in the Boy Who Lived vanquishing Lord Thingy with the power of love exteriorized on several levels in his passage through the Department of

Mysteries. The final resolution in the contest between the great contraries in the series, Gryffindor against Slytherin, ambition and pride versus selfless courage and sacrificial love, Tom Riddle, Jr., contra Albus Dumbledore, is the climax of the longest novel in the septology, the one that readers waited three years to receive.

Focusing on the structure of the journey to Harry's chrysalis in the Entry Hall, then, is only to give one of the most important scenes in the *Harry Potter* novels the attention it merits.

The Grid Chart Notes and the Actual Sequence of Rooms on Harry's Journey

As touched on above, the A, B, and C charts that Rowling has shared all point to the centrality of Harry's adventure in the Department of Mysteries. A grid column is dedicated to its foreshadowing in the boy hero's repeated travels in a near dream state to the Department throughout the book. The subplots of the attack on Mr. Weasley and Harry's subsequent Occlumency tutorial lessons with Snape all turn on these penumbral visits to the Ministry's depths via the Dark Lord's manipulations of his psyche.

The specifics of the forty-page journey, however, are as sparse as the foreshadowing is generous. The only Department of Mysteries details that are shared in the grid charts are "*Love Room*," "*Death Room*," and Sirius' death (A27; A29). It is clear from the question marks in more than one grid that, at this stage of her planning, the author had not yet worked out how the Dark Lord would entice Harry and the DA to travel to London from Hogwarts to enter the Ministry's bowels (C29). Contrast this paucity with the details of Harry's room by room travels through the Department of Mysteries:

1. After one final attempt to ditch Luna, Neville, and Ginny, Harry and five members of Dumbledore's Army enter a "*large, circular room*" where "*everything ... was black*" with walls having "*around a dozen doors.*" The room has a mind of its own, closes them off from escape, and turns out to be a carousel capable of disorienting rotation. Harry is confused because in his visions he "*had always walked purposefully across the room to the door immediately opposite the entrance*" (*Phoenix* ch. 34).

2. The first door they try opens into a "*long rectangular room*" with "*lamps hanging low on golden chains.*" It is empty "*except for a few desks*" and "*an enormous glass tank of deep green liquid*" containing "*a number of pearly-white objects ... drifting around lazily.*" Hermione identifies them as brains. There are doors in this room, but Harry elects to return to the carousel to recreate his dream experience (ch. 34).

3. After the black room spins, they pass through a door into a larger, "*dimly lit and rectangular*" room, the center of which is "*sunken, forming a great stone pit some twenty feet deep.*" The room resembles "*an amphitheater*" with a "*raised stone dais*" in the middle, on which stands an "*ancient, cracked and crumbling*" archway hung with a "*tattered black curtain or veil*" that fluttered "*very slightly.*" Harry walks around the archway, calls Sirius' name, and is disturbed to hear voices on the other side of the veil, though he can see the opposite wall through it. Luna also hears the voices, and Ginny and Neville are as "*entranced*" by the veiled archway as Harry. Hermione convinces them to leave the room and has to drag them out, considering it "*dangerous.*" They re-enter the carousel (ch. 34).

4. The door Harry tries next is locked and resists both a spoken opening-charm and Sirius' knife, the blade of which the door frame melted. Hermione convinces Harry this is not the right door because the door in his visions opened easily (ch.

34). Later, Dumbledore reveals this door opens onto a room "*kept locked at all times*" containing a force "*more wonderful and more terrible than death, than human intelligence, than the forces of nature,*" the power residing in Harry's heart (ch. 37). This is the "*Love Room*" of the grid chart notes (A27; C29).

5. The next door opens to the room of Harry's visions, one with "*beautiful, dancing, diamond-sparkling light.*" It is a menagerie of analog clocks ticking away, "*hanging in spaces between the bookcases or standing on desks.*" The light comes from a "*towering crystal bell jar ... as tall as he was,*" filled with a "*billowing, glittering wind.*" Floating at the "*heart of the bell jar*" is "*a tiny, jewel-bright egg*" from which a hummingbird emerges, rises "*to the very top of the jar,*" and then drifts to the jar's floor. As it descends, the bird's feathers "*became bedraggled and damp again*" until, at the nadir, it "*had been enclosed once more in its egg.*" This is the Time Chamber. Harry hurries his friends through the room to "*the only door behind*" the bell-jar (ch. 34).

6. They finally enter the "*very cold*" Hall of Prophecy, "*high as a church and full of nothing but towering shelves covered in small, dusty, glass orbs.*" It resembles the circular black room because of the blue light issuing from its candle-brackets. They enter at what may be the room's center, a row marked "*fifty-three,*" and move quickly to the vision destination, "*row ninety-seven.*" Sirius isn't there; no one is. Ron notices a prophecy orb with Harry's name on it, "*Dark Lord and (?) Harry Potter.*" Harry picks it up despite Hermione and Neville begging him not to, stares into it, and hears the "*drawling voice*" of Lucius Malfoy demand that he "*turn around, nice and slowly, and give that to me.*" The chapter ends here, Voldemort's trap sprung, and the battle of the Department of Mysteries begins (ch. 34).

7. Bellatrix and Lucius reveal Harry was tricked by the Dark Lord into coming to retrieve the Prophecy so he could hear its

exact wording.[2] The six DA members astonish the Death Eaters by upsetting the towering shelves of prophecy orbs and fleeing in the chaos. Ron, Ginny, and Luna head in one direction, Harry, Hermione, and Neville in another. The story narration (and several Death Eaters) follows Harry's group into the Time Room and, after a confrontation that sends a Death Eater's head into the bell-jar and seeing the "*black room*" occupied by enemies heading their way, into a "*small, dark, cluttered office*" adjoining it. Dolohov battles the trio but is petrified, though he knocks Hermione unconscious. Neville, carrying Hermione, follows Harry through the Time Room into the black circular room, now referred to as a "*black*" or "*circular hallway*" (ch. 35).

8. Ron, Luna, and Ginny rejoin them, entering the door carousel from "*a dark room full of planets*" where they spent time "*just floating in the dark.*" Ron has been hit with a Cheering Charm that makes him find everything amusing, Ginny has a severely sprained or broken ankle, and Hermione is still unconscious. Neville lifts Hermione, Luna aids Ginny, and Harry "*heaved Ron towards a door*" when "*three Death Eaters*" led by Bellatrix "*sped into the hall*" (ch. 35).

9. The door takes the three pairs of friends back into the "*Brain Room.*" Five Death Eaters enter, Luna is knocked out, and

---

[2] Harry asks the obvious question about why Voldemort didn't come to retrieve it himself; if the Prophecy is about him as well as Harry, he could touch it without consequences. Bellatrix gives the border-line ridiculous answer that he could not do this without revealing himself to the Aurors at the Ministry, though a crowd of Death Eaters has done exactly that to be there in order to take the glass orb from Harry. The entire adventure is revealed here as an artistic and symbolic artifice removed from plot necessity, one akin to the *Goblet of Fire* machinations to bring Harry to the Little Hangleton graveyard via the Triwizard Tournament trophy Portkey.

Ron foolishly lifts a brain with a Summoning Charm out of its tank, which begins to crush him with "*thin ribbons.*" Harry flees, "*holding the Prophecy high above his head,*" hoping to "*draw the Death Eaters away from the others*" (ch. 35).

10. He falls down the "*stone steps*" of the room with the veiled stone archway. He climbs "*backwards on to*" the stone dais, surrounded by ten laughing Death Eaters. Neville attempts to help Harry but is easily subdued; Bellatrix threatens to torture Longbottom as she did his parents unless Harry gives up the Prophecy. He is about to yield when five members of the Order of the Phoenix appear *ex machina* and do battle with the Death Eaters. Sirius and Lupin separately order Harry to take Neville and the Prophecy out of what the grid charts call the "*Death Room*" (A27) and Dumbledore later calls the "*Death Chamber*" (ch. 36). The Prophecy is broken as Harry and Neville climb the stairs when Dumbledore appears "*in the doorway from the Brain Room.*" As the Headmaster reels in the fleeing Death Eaters, Bellatrix hits Sirius with the killing curse that sends Harry's Godfather through the veil of the Stone Arch (ch. 35).

11. Harry chases Bellatrix back into the Brain Room and escapes the brains she spills into his path by dumping the tank of "*foul-smelling potion*" over him. He sees her disappear through a door "*in the circular black hall*" (ch. 36).

12. Harry re-enters the room, which to his frustration again becomes a "*whirling candelabra.*" He shouts "*desperately*" at the walls, "*Where's the exit? ... Where's the way out?*" The room answers as if it had "*been waiting for him to ask,*" à la the Room of Requirement. The appropriate door opens behind him, and Harry exits the Department of Mysteries (ch. 36).

The Ring Structure of Harry's Journey to the Hall of Prophecy in the Department of Mysteries

In those twelve steps, Harry and his friends enter or try to enter only seven rooms: (a) the black carousel of doors (four times), (b) the Brain Room (thrice), (c) the Death Chamber (twice), (d) they stand at the threshold of but do not enter the Love Room (once), (e) the Time Room with its adjoining office (twice), (f) the Hall of Prophecy (once), and (g) the Space Room of planets and weightlessness (once). Laid out in sequence, their journey is a – b – a – c – a (d) – e – f – e/g – a – b – c – b – a. Represented as a Mary Douglas Ring Composition circle moving from bottom to top to bottom again, the chiastic structure of latch, turn, and turtle-back lines is transparent *(see next page)*.

★ Latch in the Black Circular Hallway

Harry naturally both enters and exits the Department of Mysteries with his five side-kicks through the Department's black carousel entry room. As he enters, Harry wishes he were by himself on this mission to rescue Sirius or accompanied only by trusty Ron and Hermione but they all brush off his attempt to post them as guards at the entry; Harry exits by himself in pursuit of Sirius' killer. On entry, too, he is confused by the "*whirling candelabra*" and his inability to walk through it without difficulty to the room of his repeated visions; he exits the room easily, in contrast, when the carousel of doors seems to have become subject to his mental command.

Ring Within the Ring: Department of Mysteries Battle in *Harry Potter and the Order of the Phoenix*

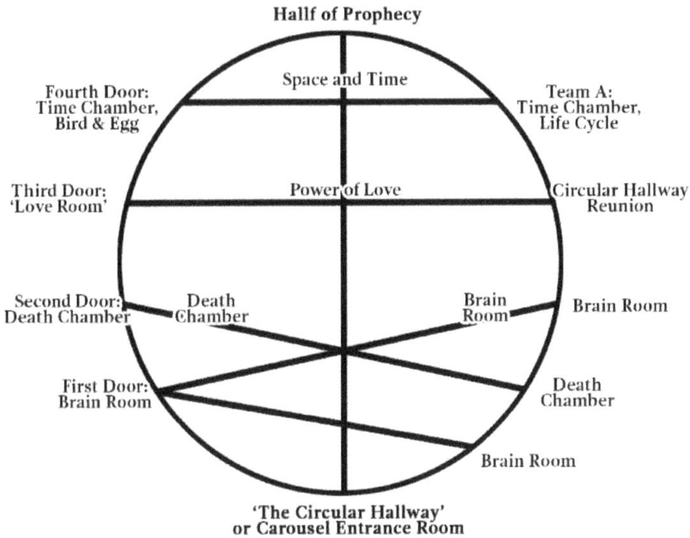

★ Turn in the Hall of Prophecy

The DA Band of Brothers try four doors and enter three rooms out of the "*circular hallway*" before finding Harry's previewed Time Room passage to the Hall of Prophecy. Harry and Company enter the same three rooms in reverse order on their way out.[3] On their twelve-step journey, the Hall is number six,

[3] There is a meaningful extra room that Ron, Luna, and Ginny enter after the six friends are separated when they flee the Death Eaters in the Hall of Prophecy and a seeming break in the reverse sequence, both of which breaks in the pure chiastic sequence will be explained below.

with five before and six after, making it the near true-center of the trip and their professed destination. The Hall of Prophecy echoes and points to the circular hallway of the beginning and end's latch in their "hall" names derived from the Anglo-Saxon word for "whole" and their predominant shape. Most of the rooms in the Department are rectangular with circular touches, e.g., the "*descending steps*" to a raised dais in the Death Room whose central feature is a semi-circular veiled "*archway*" and the Time Room's analog clock faces whose arms describe a periodic circle and whose "*towering crystal bell-jar*" with its hummingbird egg's circular cycle of life. The circular hallway, in contrast, is a proper circle that whirls so its periphery (if unmarked) is a perpetual mystery to those within it. The Hall of Prophecy, too, is defined by the glass orbs on its shelves, spheres of light with mysterious, prophetic voices trapped within each. More obviously, of course, the Hall is the turning point of the journey into the Department of Mysteries because all of the chapters before are the DA's attempts to get there to save Sirius and all the chapters after it are their efforts to escape the Death Eaters alive after learning about and gaining the Prophecy.

★ The Turtle Back Lines

As represented on the Douglas ring chart, there are four "reverse echo effect" lines between the latch and turn points at beginning, middle, and end: the two Time Room visits that bracket the Hall of Prophecy turn, the Love Room door and the reunion of friends in the circular hallway, and the trips into the Death Room and Brain Room that are the first and last rooms Harry visits on his Department of Mysteries odyssey. Starting at the top of the Douglas ring composition representation of

Harry's journey through the Department, the first turtle-back line connects the two trips he makes into the Time Room.[4]

This is a neat and obvious bracketing of the ring's turn or center in the Hall of Prophecy, as mentioned. It seems, however, on at least one count, to be a break with perfect chiastic "reverse echo" sequencing which would require the good guys to return to the Department of Mysteries entrance with stops in the Time Room, at the Love Room's door, the Death Room, and then the Brain Room, i.e., the order in which they arrived at the Hall, only backwards. Harry, Hermione, and Neville enter the Time Room out of the Hall, but Luna, Ron, and Ginny have gone "*the wrong way*" as the terrified Hermione notes (ch. 35). They ran instead into the room of planets and weightlessness or outer space; I think we are meant to think of it as the "Space Room." For reasons I will share in a moment, I do not think this was a mistake or departure from chiastic structure but a pointer to the symbolic meaning of the mysteries the Ministry has captured for close study. In brief, time and space are the "*forces of nature*" mysteries Dumbledore alludes to in his talk to Harry about love (ch. 37).[5]

The second turtle-back line from the ring representation's top or "turn" is the one connecting the DA sextet's failed

---

[4] With the exception of Harry's trips into and out of the Death Room via the Brain Room at his odyssey's end, the movement from and back to the Time Room with respect to the Hall of Prophecy is the only transition not mediated by a trip to the circular hallway.

[5] Given Rowling's proclivity for astrology, the possibility must be allowed that in addition to or instead of the complementary aspects of time and space as the core mysteries and realities of the natural world or creation, Team B's trip into the room of planets was her hat tip to the inexplicable relationship of planetary position at birth on human character and throughout life on their behaviors.

attempt to force the door to the Love Room in the circular hallway and their reunion there after their respective trips through and trials in the Time and Space Rooms. This is the least obvious of the "reverse echo" parallels but thematically perhaps the most important. It highlights the contrary motivation and perspectives of the DA members and their Death Eater foes.

The Death Eaters are only in the Department of Mysteries in slavish service to the Dark Lord. They fear his disapproval and punishment if they fail, and they look for favor and advantage should they succeed in bringing the Prophecy to their Master. They are not concerned with the well-being or even the survival of their fellow Death Eaters. The first thing Malfoy instructs them to do, in fact, in his division of the eleven members into search teams is to overlook the suffering of their mates: "*Leave Nott, leave him I say, the Dark Lord will not care for Nott's injuries as much as losing that prophecy*" (ch. 35).[6]

Harry and his friends, in contrast, are driven by love, pure and simple. Harry has been drawn to the Ministry's depth with the bait of his love for Sirius Black, his long-suffering Godfather. Once he realizes he has been duped and that Sirius is not being detained and tortured in the Hall of Prophecy, his aim shifts immediately to denying the Dark Lord what he wants, but that in the end is only his means of saving the beloved friends his mistake has brought into the Death Eaters' grasp. Though we do not learn about what is behind the Love Room door until Harry's meeting with Dumbledore back at Hogwarts, it is in

---

[6] Nott's name is chosen deliberately here, I think, to highlight the negative aspect of the Death Eater's motivation. They are *nott*, in so many words, to love their fellows as they would hope to be cared for in duress but to deny that fundamental human quality, choosing the darkness of the Dark Lord, metaphorically, over the light of everything Good.

parallel with the DA's reunion in the circular hallway because of the sacrificial love they show one another there.

Unlike what Malfoy instructs his Death Eaters, Harry ensures that none of his friends are left behind: Neville carries Hermione, Harry aids the delirious Ron, Luna acts as a crutch to Ginny with her bad ankle, and they all escape into the relative safety of the Brain Room. When the Death Eaters break into that room at last and incapacitate everyone but him and Neville, Harry raises the Prophecy high and runs into the Death Room: "*all he could think of doing was to draw the Death Eaters away from the others*" (ch. 35).[7] Harry is not only willing to help his friends; he is prepared to die sacrificially to save their lives.[8]

As readers see later in the one-on-one battle between Voldemort and Dumbledore, it is Harry's capacity for love that enables him to expel the Dark Lord when he is possessed by him. Dumbledore explicitly makes this connection between the Love Room and Harry's signature cardiac power of love in his denouement meeting with his raging student, the equivalent of the turtle-back line between this room and the DA members' self-sacrificing love for one another at their reunion in the circular hallway.

---

[7] Bellatrix exploits this defining quality in Harry, as the Dark Lord had in the bait chosen to bring him to the Hall of Prophecy, by threatening to torture Neville to death (or to insanity as she had the Longbottom parents) if Harry does not give up the glass orb they want. Only the arrival of the Order of the Phoenix stopped Harry from surrendering it to save his friend and doppelganger.

[8] The divine quality of this sacrificial love is suggested both by Dumbledore's elevation of love as the greatest power studied in the Department of Mysteries and by Sirius' sacrificial death, Black being Harry's *Godfather*.

The last two turtle-back lines on the Douglas ring chart representation connect the Brain Room and Death Room points of the DA itinerary through the mysteries at the Ministry. The lines cross one another, however, rather than run parallel to one another as in an exact chiastic sequence. Instead of a-b-c-d-c-b-a, with b and c representing the Brain and Death Rooms, the story is a-b-c-d-*b*-c-*b*-a, the Brain Room appearing before and after the Death Room instead of only after to mirror its coming before the archway on Harry's trip to the Hall of Prophecy.

I think there are at least three explanations for this ring imperfection, the first being a denial that this transposition is problematic. From this view, the ring remains intact and in perfect sequence because Harry does run from the Death Room through the Brain Room to the circular hallway in pursuit of Bellatrix. The addition of a stop in the Brain Room on Harry's way to the veiled archway is necessary for there to be a second stop in that place on his exit, i.e., if the DA pairs of three had not entered the Brain Room on the way to the Death Room but went to the Death Room directly from the circular hallway as they do on their first trip, Harry would have exited the Death Room into the whirling candelabra rather than the Brain Room, thereby breaking the chiastic sequence utterly.

On a linguistic and symbolic level, the word "chiasmus" is derived from the word for "cross." Rowling, from this view, has the ring lines cross one another to highlight playfully the ring structure of her heroes' journey. As much as Harry's flight out of the Brain Room into the Death Room is to draw the Death Eaters away from his friends, the cross symbolism of a sacrificial death à la Calvary, too, is pointed.

As interesting as those explanations are, I think the confusion or elision of the Brain and Death Rooms at the journey's entry and exit has a simpler origin and purpose. The beginning and end of the author's exploration of life's mysteries lie in her confessed obsession with *thinking* about *death* and the story's depiction of life's mysteries in exteriorized form reflects this not only in its content but in its structure. She has repeatedly said in interviews that she is preoccupied with the subject of death and doesn't understand why everyone else isn't consumed by this as well.

Rowling said in her 2012 interview with *The New Yorker* (54) that she is "*obsessed*" with "*mortality*" and "*morality*"[9]. The *Daily Mail* reported in the same year that Rowling also told a day of publication gathering she was "*obsessed by death*" and writing about it helped her with her fears:

> *Her new book The Casual Vacancy starts with a character dying and the Harry Potter author says that writing about mortality "has made me much less afraid of it."*
>
> *Speaking last night, on the day her book was released, she answered questions from 900 assembled fans at London's Queen Elizabeth Hall.*
>
> *Ms. Rowling admitted "people did die a lot in my teens" and her obsession was cemented when her mother died when she was 25.*

[9] "*I think there is a through-line [connecting* Harry Potter *and* Casual Vacancy*],*" Rowling said. "*Mortality, morality, the two things that I obsess about*" (*The New Yorker* 54). In the same press tour, she elaborated on this with Charlie Rose: "*[W]hat obsesses me -- morality, mortality, ... they run through Harry Potter completely, they run through this... I probably will never be able to write... A very, very close friend of mine, I finished the book and the first thing he said to me was how 'many people die?'. He knows me so well*" (*Charlie Rose*).

> *"Death obsesses me. I can't understand why it doesn't obsess everybody," she said.* (*Bracchi*)

These are echoes of her previous statements:

> *My books are largely about death. They open with the death of Harry's parents. There is Voldemort's obsession with conquering death and his quest for immortality at any price, the goal of anyone with magic. I so understand why Voldemort wants to conquer death. We're all frightened of it.* (*Tatler Magazine*)
>
> *In many ways, all of my characters are defined by their attitude to death and the possibility of death.* (*Today Show*)

Her thoughts about life and death, then, how human beings should live their lives and what happens to the human person at death, are, as she told Parker (*The New Yorker* 54), the "*through-line*" of her work, Potter and post-Potter.

This is not to deny or diminish the symbolism of the cross in this representation. In his discourse on love in the Headmaster's office after the battle (*Phoenix* ch. 37), Dumbledore mentions to Harry three forces that are not as "*wonderful*" or "*terrible*" as what is locked behind the Love Room door: "*death,*" "*human intelligence,*" and "*forces of nature.*" He points explicitly to the Love Room in this stirring talk to Harry about the prophesied "*power the Dark Lord knows not*" and implicitly to the Brain Room with "*intelligence,*" to the Death Chamber with "*death,*" and to the Time and the Space Rooms with "*the forces of nature,*" time and space being the metaphysical grounds of physics or natural science.[10] His conclusion contrasts the powers of individual knowledge and of self-transcending love, of mind versus that of the heart. Harry has argued that he has nothing the Dark Lord doesn't have and Harry lacks all his skills with magic; Dumbledore's response, I believe, is Rowling's conclusion about the mysteries buried beneath the Ministry: "*In the end, it mattered not that you could not close your mind. It was your heart that saved you*" (ch. 37). It is Harry's sacrificial love, Lily's great gift to him, the love of the Cross, that is simultaneously the greatest mystery of human life and the greatest human power.

Conclusion to 'Ring Within a Ring' Exegesis: So What?

The meaning of any narrative told in ring structure, according to anthropologist Mary Douglas in her *Thinking in Circles* (31–32), is found in the middle, the story turn. The meaning of Harry's trip into the Department of Mysteries, then, if Rowling is writing according to traditional formula, should be in the Hall of Prophecy.

On the level of surface narrative or plot, this is certainly true. Harry learns about the prophecy of Sybil Trelawney concerning the Dark Lord and his vanquisher, the story-behind-his-life-story heretofore unknown to him. He succeeds in keeping the Death Eaters from bringing it to Voldemort, and, according to

---

[10] There are at least twelve doors in the Department of Mysteries' circular hallway and the DA sextet only enter or attempt to enter seven rooms. Dumbledore's summary of the great "forces" in the world, though, touch on all of those rooms except the Hall of Prophecy, an understandable oversight in that his rhetorical effort with Harry at Hogwarts is all expended in an attempt to explain the meaning of a prophecy.

Dumbledore at least, he demonstrated his heroic selfless love there and throughout his odyssey which enabled him to defeat Tom Riddle, Jr., in the Ministry's entry hall. Every one of the *Harry Potter* novels are ring journeys between Privet Drive and King's Cross Station which feature a "secret center" at which mysterious place all the mysteries of the story are revealed or resolved;[11] *The Order of the Phoenix* is no exception in this. It is extraordinary in the revelation of the core narrative of the series rather than just the problems raised in the specific book.

If I were being contentious, I would say that the "meaning in the middle" of this ring structure is actually in the central turtle-back line, the one connecting the Love Room door scene and the DA reunion in the circular hallway. The heroes cannot open the door by force, by opening charm, or with a magical device, but they tap into its power on their return journey by selflessly helping one another and risking their lives to defeat what is evil. This selflessness and bravery, of course, is most evident in Sirius' gallant death, a death which is prefigured symbolically by the hummingbird death and resurrection image in the Time Room and afterwards by Fawkes' eating the Dark Lord's death curse to save Dumbledore. We see the power of love in the pairs helping one another in flight from the hallway into the Brain Room and in Harry's dash to the Death Room to save his friends, but as notably in Neville's begging (demanding?) that Harry not give up the prophecy-orb to save him from Bellatrix' torture. The young men, either of whom could have been the Chosen One according to the prophecy, mirror one another here as virtual doppelgangers in self-transcending sacrifice.

---

[11] Cf. the Mirror of Erised room "*miles*" beneath Hogwarts (*Stone* ch. 16), the Chamber of Secrets, the Shrieking Shack, the Little Hangleton graveyard, the Horcrux Island on the Cavern Lake, and King's Cross with Dumbledore's illumined shade.

Neville is one of the DA members that Harry does not want with him on this adventure – and he is the only one never to leave his side on the journey.[12]

The most important answer to the "So What?" question is found in reflection on the commonality of the mysteries the DA members encounter on their way to and from the Hall of Prophecy and how this shared ground is reflected in the chiastic structure. In a nutshell, all the mysteries they meet are resolutions of contraries as is the ring story scaffolding.

Starting again at the top, this time the very top in the Hall of Prophecy, the central mystery is prophecy itself. The Hall scene is framed by the group's entering from and exiting back into the Time room. The images of that room – the profusion of clocks, the Time Turner hourglasses, and the light-bearing "*towering crystal bell jar*" in which a life-cycle is depicted endlessly – all point to the cyclical or circular quality of time. Human experience of time, however, is caught between two delusions: quantifying it in hours despite time not being anything like matter or energy that can be truly measured—only depicted—and thinking of it as distinct categories of past, present, and future. Rowling depicts the first delusion as such in her Time Room symbols and explodes the second in the Hall of Prophecy.

The first thing about the Hall is the sheer number of prophecy orbs stored there. Harry's prophecy is shelved in row 97[13] and there are thousands of prophecies in each row.

---

[12] Harry runs away from the group in the Brain Room to save them. Despite "*inwardly praying that Neville would stay with Ron*" (*Phoenix* ch. 35), his friend promptly rejoins him in the Death Room to face the Death Eaters.

[13] The only row numbers revealed in the Hall of Prophecy are 53, Harry's point of entry out of the Time Room, and 97, his destination. These are both prime numbers, for which Rowling has something of a

Prophecy is clearly a commonplace in the Wizarding World, especially as it seems likely most are not captured into the Ministry's glass bulbs.

And what is a prophecy exactly? It is the revelation of future events in the present as if those occurrences have already happened, which is to say, as past events that can be points of reflection. A prophecy, then, is the elision of past, present, and future, an experience of eternity in which all three of the time-as-tense categories in human understanding conjoin. Prophecy is the resolution of the contraries that are the mystery of time.

Time and Space, likewise, are the polarity without duality of the natural world, mysteries that are the backdrop to all human natural science that remain impenetrable in themselves. Rowling depicts this in the split of the septet after leaving Eternity-ville into the Time and Space Rooms, the world "beneath" what is uncreated.

Love, too, is the resolution of what is perhaps the greatest contrary pair and mystery of human life, that of Self and Other.

Death is a mystery less in the sense of it having a contrary or resolvable complement, as in "left and right" or "male and female," than its being what seems to be an absolute end to what we experience in relative existence as unending. Rowling's musings about death, if her stories are reflections of her conclusions, have led her to the belief that selfless, sacrificial

---

fetish. I think the first is only a pointer to Harry's having arrived at the center, 53 being halfway to 97, but the latter, being the highest two-digit prime number and being the numerologically significant 9 or 3^2 and 7, means he has arrived at the alocal place or heart of the Hall, the secret center where all things will be revealed.

love is the means to victory over death, the passage to immortality.[14]

And "intelligence," the mystery represented in the Brain Room? This is the mystery of epistemology, which is to say, how we know anything. The delusion is that knowledge is a function of brain chemistry, though no known fact or human cognitive ability has ever been isolated in a chemical compound or nerve cell.[15] If I am right in what I have written in other places about Rowling's familiarity with and acceptance of the English High Fantasy tradition's tenet derived from the work of Samuel Taylor Coleridge, than the mystery of knowledge, as with the others in this ring-within-the-ring of *Phoenix*, is also a resolution of contraries, namely, that of knowing subject and known object. Coleridge, after the German Romantics and Eastern Christian saints, postulated that the *logos* within each person is the means of our knowing anything because of this extra-personal faculty's ability to recognize the *logoi* in every created thing, a coincidence of subject and object akin to that of our recognition of self in a mirror.[16]

---

[14] Hence her use of mother's love as her go-to symbolism for the love of Christ (cf. the several *Hogwarts Professor* posts on this subject) and the ghosts who appear to Harry on his *Deathly Hallows* walk into the Forbidden Forest to meet his own death (ch. 34), all of whom chose to die in order to save Harry.

[15] Identification of the brain parts in which certain activities happen predominantly if never exclusively is not the same thing as isolation of thought or knowledge in a material substance or organ's cells.

[16] For the Estecean epistemology, see James Cutsinger's *The Form of the Transformed Vision: Coleridge and the Knowledge of God*; for its relevance to understanding *Harry Potter*, see my *Deathly Hallows Lectures*, "The Seeing Eye," on the meaning of mirror symbolism in Rowling's Wizarding World books.

If I am correct in noting that all of Rowling's mysteries, those in the Department and noted later by Dumbledore, are resolutions of contraries, the importance of her choice to write her series, novels, and important scenes as chiastic pieces or rings becomes especially meaningful. As I explained in "How does 'Ring Composition' Work Anyway?" at *Hogwarts Professor*, the symbolism of the circle or sphere as with the cross is the revelation of the otherwise invisible defining or creative center-point, the so-called "origin" in both sacred geometry and Cartesian graphing.[17] More important than the revelation of this origin is the *experience* of it in the human imagination, which per Coleridge again and English fantasy tradition consequent to him, is the logos within us, i.e., that creative principle recognizing its reflection in story and symbol.

The ring-within-the-ring of *Order of the Phoenix*, Harry Potter's chiastic journey through the Department of Mysteries, then, with all its symbolic representation of life's essential mysteries, each of which is answered by a depiction of the resolution of contraries into the One or Absolute, to include love's victory over death, is structure not only reflecting theme and meaning but being a vehicle for its sure delivery to the reader. Having suspended disbelief and entered her story imaginatively, with the transpersonal heart or *logos*, the reader experiences the metaphysical center in this self-contained ring laden with images of circles and cycles, from the "*whirling*

---

[17] See Eliade's *The Myth of the Eternal Return* and *The Two and the One* as well as Guenon's *The Symbolism of the Cross* for the symbolism of the circle and the cross. See my *Deathly Hallows Lectures*, "The Seeing Eye," for the meaning of Harry's King Cross meeting with Dumbledore. See my discussion of the symbolism of the circle and the cross in Rowling's finest work to date, *Troubled Blood*, at *Hogwarts Professor*.

candelabra" of the "*circular hallway*" and the analog clock faces in the Time Room to the veiled archway of Death, and the illuminating bell-jar containing life and death, all of which symbolism the side-to-side echoing and top-to-bottom parallelism of the ring story scaffolding duplicates and delivers simultaneously. The structure of this ring of all Rowling's rings depicts the meaning of her story, perhaps all imaginative fiction, the experience of the Center or cosmic *Logos* by the human inner essence or small lambda *logos*.

Conclusion To the Grid Chart Thesis

To circle back to my essay's starting point, my argument has been that the grid charts of Rowling's plot points for *The Order of the Phoenix* are valuable only to the manuscript historian whose aim is to track a work's transformation from inspiration to publication. To make that point I have illustrated how much of Rowling's structural artistry is nowhere reflected in the A, B, and C charts, most notably, in their not showing the artistry and meaning of Rowling's ring within the *Phoenix* ring. The marriage in this last between the chiastic structure and Rowling's esoteric meaning both with respect to life's mysteries and the human experience of the transcendent in story is perhaps the singular height in the *Harry Potter* novels. None of that is evident or even suggested in the grid notes about Harry's rescue mission odyssey with five DA members into the Department of Mysteries.

When F. Scott Fitzgerald died in December 1940, he left drafted chapters and outlined notes for a book tentatively titled *The Last Tycoon*. Incredibly, these first drafts and notes were "edited" and expanded by Edward Wilson into a book with the same title that was published in 1941, a work that is now considered the author's last novel.

This is *prima facie* absurd and something like a crime. Fitzgerald made his money writing for the 'slicks,' over one hundred and sixty short stories of various length and quality. His novels, however, were endlessly rewritten and revised before publication so they only vaguely resemble their first drafts and outlines. He was an alcoholic whose career is largely an icon of wasted talent lost to drink and a neurotic spouse, but the genius and artistry of *Gatsby* and *Tender is the Night* did not suffer from lack of attention and careful revisions (not to mention the guidance of Scribner's editor Maxwell Perkins).

I bring up *The Last Tycoon* to make an obvious point about *The Order of the Phoenix*. Rowling is a great planner; she has said many times that her care in planning is the secret to her success and that she revisited and revised the plans of her later *Harry Potter* novels for six months before actually writing them. Taking the grid charts for *Phoenix* seriously means taking her first plot point notes as meaningful. Though as I hope I've demonstrated, even as structure outlines, they reflect little of Rowling's story organization magic in its various dimensions.

While I admire the care with which these charts have been analyzed, dated, and organized into three parts, I confess to thinking that the finished work is what the serious reader should always be referring to in their discussion of Rowling's craft and freight. Her genius as a novelist is not in her plots or characters, I would argue, but in her use of embedded symbolism and myth and a ring structure that delivers her traditional meaning, little to none of which is in play in her early charting of the novel.

Works Cited

Bracchi, Paul. "What Is JK Rowling's Obsession with Death? Author Reveals Her Dark Side and Why the Subject Helps Her Deal with Mortality." *Daily Mail*, 27 Sept. 2012.

Cutsinger, James S. *The Form of Transformed Vision: Coleridge and the Knowledge of God.* Mercer University Press, 1988.

Douglas, Mary. *Thinking in Circles: An Essay on Ring Composition.* Yale University Press, 2007.

Eliade, Mircea. *The Myth of the Eternal Return: Or, Cosmos and History.* Princeton University Press, 1971.

———. *The Two and the One.* University of Chicago Press, 1979.

Fitzgerald, F. Scott. *The Last Tycoon.* Charles Scribner's Sons, 1941.

Granger, John. *The Deathly Hallows Lectures.* Zossima Press, 2008. Chapter 5, "The Seeing Eye: Deathly Hallows' Eye and Mirror Symbolism," pp. 151–190.

———. *Harry Potter as Ring Composition and Ring Cycle.* Lulu, 2010.

———. "How does 'Ring Composition' Work, Anyway?" *Hogwarts Professor*, 19 Nov. 2010.

———. "Ring Composition." *Hogwarts Professor*, 25 Dec. 2018.

Guénon, René. *The Symbolism of the Cross.* 1931. Sophia Perennis et Universalis, 2001.

Rowling, J.K. Interview by Charlie Rose. *Charlie Rose*, 19 Oct. 2012.

———. Interview by Geordie Greig. "There would be so much to tell her..." *Tatler Magazine*, February 2006, pp. 128–35.

———. Interview by Ian Parker. "Mugglemarch: J.K. Rowling writes a realist novel for adults." *The New Yorker*, 1 October 2012, pp. 52–63.

———. Interview by Meredith Vieira. "JK Rowling One-On-One" *Today Show*, NBC, 27 July 2007.

PATRICIO TARANTINO

The Grid as a Fundamental Clue

Speculating the Impact of the Leaked Plans in an Alternative Timeline, and How the Fandom Would Have Tried to Interpret It

Ah, the *Harry Potter* fandom during the years when the books were being published. One doesn't want to fall into the trap of becoming that grumpy old person who insists that everything was better in the good old days, but it's undeniable that there was something magical about that era. No, we're not talking about Hogwarts magic, but rather the magic of anticipation, speculation, and the community that formed around J.K. Rowling's saga. Would it be possible to sit ourselves in that universe, that moment of the timeline, and theorize what could have happened if the plans for *The Order of the Phoenix* had leaked at the time, before the release of the book?

It was a time when each day brought the possibility of a new revelation. Especially between the publication of the fifth and seventh books, the wizarding world seemed to be constantly expanding, not just through the pages of the books, but also on the big screen with the film adaptations. Fans lived in a state of constant excitement, alternating between devouring available information and wildly speculating about what would come next.

Social media was still in its infancy, but internet forums were buzzing with activity. Every snippet of an interview with Rowling, every behind-the-scenes photo, every rumor about the next book was analyzed with a fervor worthy of the most dedicated scholars. It was as if an entire generation of readers had turned into a less sinister version of Rita Skeeter, looking for clues and connections in the most unexpected places.

But perhaps the most exciting part of this whole experience was the theories. Based on fragments from the books, cryptic statements from Rowling, and sometimes pure imagination, fans built elaborate hypotheses about the future of the saga. Some were far-fetched, others surprisingly accurate, but all were a testament to how deeply readers had immersed themselves in the world of *Harry Potter*.

One theory, in particular, was etched into my personal memory.[1] Long before the publication of the sixth book, when we were still trying to process the events of the Department of Mysteries, a bold idea emerged: Harry had a fragment of Voldemort's soul inside him. This theory was based on a series

---

[1] I can't find this specific theory now, but see "Harry and Voldemort", *Harry Latino* for an example of a similar post.

of clues scattered throughout the books, but one of the most convincing came from *The Chamber of Secrets*. In that book, when Harry sees Tom Riddle's name, he feels a strange familiarity, as "*as though Riddle was a friend he'd had when he was very small, and half-forgotten*" (*Chamber* ch. 13) In hindsight, this connection seems obvious, but at the time, it was a shocking revelation.

The theory went further, connecting dots that seemed unrelated: Harry's ability to speak Parseltongue, his mental connection with Voldemort through dreams, even the way Voldemort's wand reacted in the graveyard at the end of *The Goblet of Fire* (ch. 34). Although some of the evidence presented might not have been entirely correct or relevant, the final conclusion turned out to be astonishingly accurate.

These types of theories weren't just a hobby for fans; they also seemed to have an impact on the author herself. J.K. Rowling has admitted on several occasions that some people had guessed or come very close to guessing the end of the saga: "*They have such fun with their theories ... and it is fun, it is fun. And some of them even get quite close*" (*BBC Newsnight*).[2] This statement raises a fascinating fact: Rowling read internet theories. The idea of the author browsing fan forums, perhaps laughing at some far-fetched theories and nervously biting her nails at others that were surprisingly accurate, adds an additional layer of fun to the whole phenomenon.

However, the theories that were correct were not the norm but the exception. Most of them were fabrications that never came true — which was logical and natural, given how many

[2] In this same interview, prior to the release of book five, J.K. Rowling was directly asked about Snape having had a crush on Harry's mother, something that wouldn't be revealed until the final book.

there were; if they had all been true, the books would have had to be hundreds of thousands of pages long (and full of contradictions, of course). Perhaps the most popular among all the failed ones was the one that even had its own website: *DumbledoreIsNotDead.com* (Haber). Despite the justifications and evidence it presented, Albus Dumbledore was indeed dead. And what happened with this theory was the same as with many others: the theory writers started with the conclusion, with what they wanted to happen, and then worked backward, trying to find evidence or clues to support their original thesis, even discarding those that might contradict it. Obviously, these theories and the subsequent discussions were carried out with the utmost seriousness, as if investigating a real crime, when in reality, they were far from being anything serious.

While Rowling had not yet written the future books at the times fans were theorizing about them, she had planned them out in her notes. Most of these notes are things we've only since seen glimpses of or heard about second hand. For the fifth book, however, her outline has since been published, and we can now see what her early notes had looked like. Looking at this outline for *The Order of the Phoenix*, an intriguing question arises: if by some twist of fate, the detailed plan for the fifth book had leaked before its publication, how far could Potterheads have gone in their deductions? Would they have been able to decipher the entire book? Are there aspects that the plan, by its very nature, doesn't reveal? And perhaps most excitingly, would it have provided clues about the two following books?

To answer the questions we're posing, we need to enter a realm almost as fantastic as J.K. Rowling's books themselves. Perhaps even play with a special Time-Turner (à la *Cursed Child*) that allows us to see an alternate timeline. So, the first step would be to imagine the origin of these parallel events. As we know, the first page of the outline was revealed on the author's website in 2006, after the publication of the sixth book. This website, remembered by fans of the time for its creativity and unique designs, was created by the company Lightmaker.[3]

The design studio (which no longer exists) was known for designing and developing celebrity websites, such as that of footballer Wayne Rooney. To create Rowling's website, they had privileged access to many of her things: not only material that appeared on the page (such as manuscripts or illustrations), but also access to her desk, house (at least through photos), and more (to recreate it in the interactive environment that was the site's navigation). And among all these things, they had access to part of the *Order of the Phoenix* grid.

Let's imagine then, in this game we're playing, that the Lightmaker team asks Rowling for the complete grid shortly after she created it, with the excuse that they will evaluate which are the best pages to share on the website after the book is published. Rowling then sends them all. Later, Lightmaker scans all the pages and, to share them among their team and also with the author's own team (to receive feedback and so on), uploads them to a private section of the website. So far, all plausible and nothing out of this world. The twist that will open the door to this new timeline is the obsessive characteristic of the *Harry Potter* fan.

While it's true that in the years that Rowling's "desktop" website (as it was remembered) lasted there were no hacks or leaks, Rowling's fans did try. They tried so vehemently that there have even been fake videos simulating opening the

---

[3] Evanna Lynch, who played Luna Lovegood in the Harry Potter films, mentioned this website and her experience of visiting it as a fan before she was cast. That experience is recollected in her foreword for the digital book *From the Wizarding Archive*.

famous door that hid secrets (this video suggested that the title of the sixth book was going to be titled "Pillar of Storgé").[4] It was never known for certain if the impossibility of hacking/leaking was because Lightmaker handled the website's security very well, or simply because there was nothing to hack: what was public was all there was.[5]

So mixing these repeated attempts and the existence of this grid on the web server, we can assume the scenario we're looking for: *Harry Potter* fans obtain the *Order of the Phoenix* plan before its publication. And then?

What follows is pure speculation (because our Time-Turner hasn't yet reached our hands) about the fandom's initial reaction and their subsequent "use" of it: how fans would have theorized about the available material and how far they would have gone. This exercise will also try to imitate what we said about the theories earlier: some will be correct and others won't, and we will also try to start with our final thesis and see if we can prove it by looking at the grid.

The first thing the fans would look at would be the column titles that precede the table. Obviously the first three are easy

---

[4] Although developed years later, the Pottermore websites were not spared from tech-savvy fans and also suffered leaks, which allowed access to J.K. Rowling's writings before their official release, access to unused concept art, and even the names of the Ilvermorny houses before they were officially shared.

[5] Another consideration that must be made is that the "desktop website" would have needed to launch much earlier than it actually did. Lightmaker didn't release it until 2004, the year after *Order of the Phoenix* was published. In this alternate timeline, not only would they have needed to make some security mistakes, but they also would have had to have completed the website more than a year before it was actually completed.

to understand: chapter number, time setting, and title. Then each header defines the subplot that will be detailed later, with a main "*Plot*" that will set the pace.

Hagrid Relationship

Let's start with the end. The last column is titled "*Hagrid and Grawp*", and with the background of *Goblet of Fire*, where there are glimpses of a potential romantic life for Hagrid, it's not difficult to think that's what the fans would have imagined. The column details that Hagrid spends a lot of time with the giants (C1-C9), then that he returns with Grawp (C11), that he gets mysterious injuries (B13-20; C12-20), and that afterwards he refuses to abandon Grawp (B24; C25). At no point in the column is "him" or "her" mentioned to refer to the new character, so it would be completely natural to assume that it could be a Hagrid romantic partner. It could also be considered a closure or expansion on the topic of giants and half-giants, a theme introduced in the fourth book. While this is the case with the Grawp plot, it is a different type of relationship that we see with Hagrid. However, it's not just at the column level where there is information about this. Some fans (I imagine debates in forums lasting for days) will notice that the chapter titles also provide information. And one of them is called "*Cousin Grawp*" (B22; C22), precisely the one where the Plot says that the trio meets this new character. After this gets pointed out, there will be a pivot in the attempt to guess what happens, and many fans will believe (with certainty) that Grawp is not a romantic interest of Hagrid but simply a cousin of his. Of course, those attached to the original theory will try to find justifications: that "Cousin" might be a first name used within the giant community, or even maybe a familiar title,[6] that it's the way Hagrid introduces him to avoid drawing attention, or some might even justify it by saying that relationships between relatives might be allowed in the giant community due to their wild nature (personally, I can't imagine J.K. Rowling doing that, but we know that fans can get defensive to the point of suggesting such things). The truth is that no one would have guessed correctly because the published version, although very similar, shows Grawp as Hagrid's half-brother (and far from being a romantic interest).

Ginny and Cho Chang

Let's also consider that there is another column that talks about a potential love relationship (and this is completely confirmed, because we know the characters): it is the one about "*Cho and Ginny.*" So if we consider that Rowling decided to give them a column for that relationship, it would not be at all strange for her to do the same for Hagrid. But since we are in the column of Miss Chang and Weasley, let's see what Rowling planned for them. And what we see is very similar to the final book. There is no mystery: the fans with access to this would see the ups and downs of Harry's relationship with the Ravenclaw student, with a little information about Ginny, who was a bit worried about her father (B16, C16) and growing and having her own relationships (B17,19; C17,19). We even know that something would happen with her and Seamus Finnigan, or at least the author was already considering it (C17,19).

---

[6] Similar to how the wizard Gandalf refers to his colleague Radagast as "*cousin*" in *The Hobbit* (Tolkien ch. 7), despite not being blood relatives.

The Order of the Phoenix

And in the column of the Ravenclaw student, Cho Chang, there is a small detail that will solve a mystery: the phrase "*Cho wants to join Order of the Phoenix*" (C13) will give meaning to the book's title.[7] Let us remember that the title was revealed in October 2000 (just months after the release of the fourth book and almost three years before the fifth). It was first during a TV show, where the author told a child (*Today Show*), and later in the afternoon, during an online chat organized by a bookstore (*Barnes & Noble*). But even knowing it was going to be called *The Order of the Phoenix*, what did it mean? No one was sure that *The Order of the Phoenix* was an organization, as the title could have other meanings. "*Order*" could be a command (a rather imperative phoenix, if you will), or even a noun related to peace and control, suggesting something like "a phoenix was called to restore order". (The "phoenix" in these cases might of course not be a literal phoenix, and could instead be a metaphor for another character or some entity). But Cho's simple desire clears up the doubt and confirms that the Order of the Phoenix is an organization and that Harry's love interest wants to join it.

Having this information, (I imagine a thread in some fan forum titled "Confirmation of the Meaning of the HP5 Title," with the subsequent explanation), it is easier to try to understand the column under the label "*OP*." What we can read there talks about an initial idea (C12), then recruiting (B13; C13), and then several meetings (B14-24; C14-26), with the occasional reference to these meetings taking place in corridors

[7] In the outline "*Order of the Phoenix*" is usually abbreviated as "*OP*" or "*O of P*", but there are a few places where it is written out in full in ways that are directly connected to the abbreviation (e.g. B14).

(C25-26). Adding to this the fact that it relates the Order of the Phoenix to Fred and George, and the fact that "*things*" were "*hotting up*" for them (B24), we can assume that this organization takes place at Hogwarts and that students are involved. The fact that Fred and George are the only ones appearing in that column may lead us to believe that it is an organization only "available" to the older students at the school — even the phrase "*things hotting up*" could have a double meaning, and the idea that Cho Chang would want to join could reinforce this idea. However, it would be strange for an organization like this (perhaps somewhat similar to the Slug Club that appears in the next book) to be the title of the novel. There is a detail we are overlooking, or at least any attentive fan should think so.

But we can't blame the fans: the Plot column (perhaps the most important one) also mentions the Order, and, on one hand, reinforces the idea. It's an organization that is "*being hunted*" or "*suspected by Umbridge*" (who is she?), and that makes its importance such that its members miss Quidditch matches (B20; C20). What could be so interesting for teenagers? It's in a 2001 interview where perhaps Rowling gave a possible answer (which fans could use to justify one of the possible and strange goals of the student association Order of the Phoenix): "*There's more boy-girl stuff. They're 15 now, hormones working overtime. Harry has to ask some questions, that I hope the reader will think: 'well, why hasn't he asked this before?'*" (*Harry Potter and Me*).

Another key reference to this organization also appears in the Plot column: "*discovery of the Order of the Phoenix - Dumbledore takes the rap ... Azkaban.*" (B23; C23) It seems that this organization is finally discovered, Dumbledore takes responsibility, and ends up in Azkaban. Wow! This organization must be doing something very wrong for the punishment to be that severe. It can't be anything related to teenage hormones... and if we keep looking at that column, we also see that the Golden Trio is recruiting for the organization (B13; C13). So unless we get very imaginative, we can discard the original idea.

But then what would this Order of the Phoenix be? We know that it's a teenage organization, operating almost in secret at Hogwarts, hunted by someone named Umbridge, and that when it's discovered, Dumbledore takes responsibility and ends up in Azkaban. This last detail might give us a clue: the one authorized to sentence someone to Azkaban is the Ministry of Magic. Is the Order of the Phoenix an association that goes against it? We know from the end of the fourth book that one thing that bothers the Minister is the spreading of the news of Voldemort's return (*Goblet* ch. 36). Surprisingly though, we don't see a lot of mention of this in the outline. Perhaps this was the plot thread that meant to address this, with the Order of the Phoenix's goal being to spread Dumbledore's word and try to convince others that You-Know-Who's return is true.

Does this fit what we "learned" about the Order? It makes sense that Fred and George are part of it, and that Harry, Ron, and Hermione recruit people as well. That Cho Chang wants to join doesn't seem far-fetched, but quite the opposite: Voldemort killed her ex-boyfriend, so a certain desire for revenge would be rational. Dumbledore taking responsibility wouldn't be out of place either, because after all, he is one of the leaders of the fight against the Dark Lord.

And if we pay attention to the grid with a more general view, we can notice that there's something connecting Hagrid with this group, which is that Umbridge seems to be concerned about both. Someone might quickly make the following association: Hagrid helps Harry with the idea of spreading the news of Lord

Voldemort's return, and that's what he was doing with the giants: he went to tell them that Voldemort is back.

And while that conclusion would be correct (that does end up happening in the book), let's stop for a second and try to recap. Because although the conclusion is true, what precedes it is not: that is not the function of the Order of the Phoenix (and it doesn't even end up being called that in the final book). Moreover, making that association isn't feasible: Hagrid is with the giants already in the first chapters, long before "*Idea for Order of the Phoenix*" appears in the grid (C12).

Dolores Umbridge

There is a connection in these errors, and it's the name Umbridge. Unfortunately, we didn't know who she was before the book's publication.[8] So the fandom could only speculate about her supposed identity. Many rumors placed Lupin and Lockhart as possible returns for the DADA position (following the custom of having a new DADA professor in each new year/book, especially considering the fact that Crouch Jr was kissed, and a new person was now needed for the position). Although Lupin and Lockhart do appear in the previous books, that wasn't their role. And any sensible fan, knowing that the DADA position is important to the book's plot, would know that if one of these two characters were to fill that role, they would appear in the insufferable know-it-all grid as professors, which is not the case, so they could have been ruled out.

[8] A handwritten card by J.K. Rowling stating she was the new Defense Against the Dark Arts professor was auctioned in December 2002 ("Autograph Card Signed"), but its contents were not revealed at the time, and we only learned that it contained Dolores Umbridge's identity in 2019.

But there's no need to beat around the bush: the grid mentions *"Professor Umbridge"* or *"first Umbridge lesson"* several times (C7; C8; C9), which would lead anyone to the most obvious option. Knowing then the name of the new DADA professor, what else can we know about her?

We know that she moves furtively (*"Umbridge skulking"* [C10]) and that she complains about them visiting Hagrid (*"Umbridge complaint they went"* [C11]).[9] It might seem crazy knowing the future and what happened afterwards, but does it really sound so far-fetched that Umbridge could be a professor secretly watching Harry and company under Dumbledore's orders? Similar to what Mrs. Figg would later do, since Dumbledore can't do it himself because he's being watched by the Ministry of Magic, although of course at that time before the book's release, that wouldn't have been known. This theory would be somewhat correct, but with the wrong character and context.

This could be a completely valid theory about the role Umbridge was going to play in this fifth book. Furthermore, following the theory that the *Harry Potter* books are mirrored, the Defense Against the Dark Arts professor in the fifth book should mirror the professor in the third book, who is Remus Lupin and ends up being an ally to Harry. Another fact from the grid is that Umbridge would be introduced in the Hogwarts Express (C7), which would mirror what happened with Moony (*Azkaban* ch. 5).

---

[9] There is also the phrase *"Umbridge warden to Dumbledore"* (C12), but as people who wrote theories used to do, we will ignore it because it doesn't serve our purpose.

Dumbledore's Army

Speaking of Lupin, he also appears in a column we've yet to pay attention to: "*DA*" Here, he's associated with his close friend Sirius Black (the return of the lost godfather) and a new character named Tonks. Who is this new character? A phrase from the row of Chapter 23 ("*Treason*") gives us several answers: "*He won't fight because Tonks is here, and if she supports, he'll blow DA*" (C23).[10]

The first thing this tells us is that Tonks is a female character. The entire grid places great importance on the emotional relationships between characters—and while Hagrid's theorizing was wrong, Ginny and Cho's wasn't. Even die-hard fans would likely have agreed that Tonks was going to be a love interest for Lupin, if we look at the cell that says "*Tonks and Lupin*" (B13; C13).

But the other important thing that sentence tells us is that "DA" is something that should be kept secret. What could be the meaning of "DA"? In the cell for Chapter 13 ("*Plots and Resistance*"), we can see the meaning of those initials (and how the media could blow the secret too): "*Daily Prophet story about Dumbledore's Army*" (C13). And what will this "Army" be? A synonym for what Dumbledore calls "*the old crowd*" at the end of *Goblet*: "*Sirius, I need you to set off at once. You are to alert Remus Lupin, Arabella Figg, Mundungus Fletcher—the old crowd*" (*Goblet* ch. 36). And although Mundungus Fletcher doesn't appear in these plans, Mrs. Figg does, reinforcing the idea that this "*old crowd*" could be what is referred to here as "*Dumbledore's Army*". And while we now know this theory was

---

[10] Unlike other shorthand used in this outline, it would not have been immediately clear what "*DA*" stood for.

wrong, it's not the fault of the fans but of J.K. Rowling for changing the name of the secret organization. Had the author made that decision from the beginning, it would have been much easier to correctly associate the members with the Order of the Phoenix.

But what is the role of this group of adult witches and wizards under the command of the Headmaster of Hogwarts?

To Protect Harry

It's obvious that the return of Lord Voldemort means one thing: Harry Potter is in constant danger. And Dumbledore can do nothing but protect him. That's why he gathers his old guard to form his own army, tasked with protecting the only wizard who survived the Avada Kedavra curse and who holds the key to defeating the Dark Lord. Why do we assume this is the mission of Dumbledore's Army? From what we can infer from some of the cells.

Lupin, Tonks, and Moody take Harry to Grimmauld Place (C3), where Dumbledore's Army meets for the first time and decides on its objectives (C4). Afterward, someone is interrogated at the Ministry of Magic (C5), and throughout this Harry isn't mentioned at all for three chapters (C4-C6). One way to understand this is that Harry doesn't make decisions for himself: he's taken from place to place, following orders, being protected without much freedom. On the train, Rowling notes that people are giving Harry a "*wide berth*" (C7): could Dumbledore's Army be preventing anyone from getting close to him? Other phrases suggest similar ideas: "*Dumbledore's Army hanging around him*" (C11). But is it really Voldemort that Harry is being protected from? The grid is unclear about Voldemort's plans, and while fans might imagine that the Dark

Lord's ultimate plan is to kill the boy who lived, perhaps the heir of Salazar Slytherin has something else in mind. Is it possible to imagine anything—right or wrong—using this grid?

Voldemort's Goal

To understand Voldemort's objectives, there's a column we haven't used yet titled "*Prophecy*," and in its very first cell (C1), there's something that tells us to pay attention if we want to know what the Dark Lord is up to: "*Voldemort plotting but badly informed*." Voldemort is not only already planning, but he also has informants. Much has happened since the end of the fourth book, where he gained a body: now he has a team of (predictable) people investigating for him. The next sentence, "*thinks anyone can take*," which alludes to the "*badly informed*," tells us there's something to take. However, "*take*" can mean many things: taking, enduring, accepting, assuming, understanding, and more. If we take the column title as a reference, it would be "take the prophecy," which still doesn't clarify much. Let's continue.

The references following after that talk about the Ministry of Magic, and how Lucius and Bode are trying to cautiously approach something, with Bode even seeming to be aware that "*on some level he can't do it*" (C7). Then comes the clarification of "*take*": "*Voldemort impatiently awaits Bode's theft but it is very difficult*" (C8). Voldemort wants something stolen... a prophecy?

The column continues telling us that there are more attempts and that even Dumbledore's Army is hanging around it, as if they also wanted to get hold of the prophecy. Let's remember that the theory fans have been building in this alternative timeline had suggested that Dumbledore's Army's project, their objective, was to spread the news of Lord Voldemort's return. And now we're assuming that there's a prophecy that Voldemort wants to steal, and it seems that Dumbledore's Army also wants to get it. Is there a possibility then that this prophecy is the one Trelawney makes in the third book, and that Voldemort wants to keep it hidden to continue working in the shadows? While if the Army gets it, it will help them with their ultimate goal?

The "*Prophecy*" column continues to give us a bit more information: Harry having visions (C8) and a Hall of Prophecies (C13). While the second doesn't seem to tell us much, we can make a twisted explanation of the first (which, remember, was how most fan theories were in those years). Harry was the only witness to Trelawney's prophecy in the third book (*Azkaban* ch. 16). Could these visions be related to that? Could it be the way the prophecy is "stored," through Harry's memory (Pensieve, anyone?), and the way it's retrieved is through these visions? Considering that Voldemort seems to want to bring Harry there, perhaps this Hall of Prophecies isn't a real place, but an imaginary one (à la King's Cross in the seventh book), where Harry must go to retrieve Trelawney's prophecy to bring it to the real plane (too far-fetched, I know).

The Ending

The whirlwind of the final chapters — at least as we know them now — isn't entirely clear following the grid. As we near the end, the details get more sparse and the outline gets more linear, making it easier to follow just the main plot. Based on this, we know that Snape won't teach anymore because Harry saw his worst memory (A23; C25). Does Snape have his own Pensieve? Then it seems this triggers Hagrid getting sacked

(C26), Fred and George getting expelled (C26), a breakout in Azkaban (A25; C27), and Voldemort managing to break through to what he was seeking (A25; C28). Is it too far-fetched to think that because Harry saw this about Snape, Snape feels so offended that he decides to betray Harry, and consequently Dumbledore? Any fan with this grid wouldn't take long to make that connection and think about why Snape's anger facilitates Voldemort starting to fulfill his objective.

Somehow (perhaps Harry sees something else in Snape's Pensieve?), our protagonist travels on horseback toward where Voldemort is (pursued by Dementors), and arrives at the Ministry of Magic, hidden under his cloak (A25-26; C28). This last detail makes us assume Harry would go alone, because how would others hide if they accompany him? But the use of plural in the grid, "*they fight way in*" (A26), seems to contradict this. So, does only Harry hide?

What follows appears to be a sequence similar to the first book (*Stone* ch. 16), crossing different places/rooms: "*death room,*" "*love room,*" and others, until the Death Eaters and "*Sirius and Co*" arrive (A27-28; C30). Unfortunately, there's little room for doubt: Sirius seems to be the character who finally dies, choosing that fate instead of the Dementors (A29). The next line is very interesting: "*Hermione and Ron pull Harry back from death*" (A30). Will we then see a scene where Harry dies? The following seems to confirm this, as it says Voldemort goes crazy because of this. Finally, Ministry Wizards arrive and Voldemort flees, but we have in the next chapter an explanation of everything that happened from Dumbledore (A31). Again, similarities with *The Philosopher's Stone* (ch. 17).

While details are missing, theorizing about the ending based on the grid is quite possible and there isn't much room for doubt. However, we only know the facts: not their real meanings, or their possible consequences. But we can say that "the ending of *The Order of the Phoenix*" emerges from the grid and is where Rowling had a clearer vision. Which makes absolute sense: it's where everything must fit faithfully, as the objective of planning is to reach that instance without leaving loose ends. And albeit different in some significant details, a clear and well-explained ending in a grid translates to a clear and well-explained ending in the novel.

Conclusion

The grid that J.K. Rowling used doesn't contain the entire story of the book, of course. In a philosophical debate, we might even ask ourselves if the physical book contains the whole story, or if it's simply the words that allow our minds, through imagination, to fill in the rest. But we could ask whether the grid contains the minimal but yet sufficient information to develop the rest of the story from it. Playing the role of the obsessive *Harry Potter* fans of the early 2000s, who theorized what might happen based on small passages from the books, we put ourselves in their shoes and tried to show that it's just as easy to be wrong as it is to be right. The grid works as a fundamental piece of the book, but it's far from sufficient. It does allow, with a bit of luck, for future events to be guessed, connected with passages from the first four books, and to visualize where the plot is headed. But it's almost impossible to do so in its entirety because there are gaps—either because Rowling hadn't yet decided on them or because she didn't consider them important enough to write down. Without them there was no way to connect the events mentioned in the plan coherently.

So, this exercise of taking a (cheating) time-turner and going back more than 20 years can show us that the grid for *The Order of the Phoenix* is, as mathematicians say when talking about the relationship between two statements, a "necessary but not sufficient" condition to write the great work that is the fifth novel of the *Harry Potter* saga.

Works Cited

ChicoStroke. "Harry and Voldemort are one and the same, because Voldemort did not die" *Harry Latino*, 2 Aug, 2004.

Haber, Dave. "Dumbledore Clues." *DumbledoreIsNotDead*, 19 July 2005.

Lynch, Evanna. Foreword. *From the Wizarding Archive: Curated Writing from the World of Harry Potter*, by J.K. Rowling, Pottermore Publishing, 2024.

Rowling, J.K. "Autograph Card Signed ('J.K. Rowling') Referring to the Forthcoming Book *Harry Potter and the Order of the Phoenix*." Partially reproduced in *English Literature, History, Private Press & Children's Books*, Sotheby's, 12 Dec. 2002, lot 517, p. 229.

———. Interview. *Harry Potter and Me*. BBC, 28 Dec. 2001.

———. Interview by Jeremy Paxman. *BBC Newsnight*, BBC Two, 19 June 2003.

———. Interview by Katie Couric. Today Show. NBC, 20 Oct. 2000.

———. Webchat with Barnes & Noble. *barnesandnoble.com*. 20 Oct. 2000.

Tolkien, J.R.R. *The Hobbit*. George Allen & Unwin, 1937.

Appendix A: The Outline

As described in the introduction ("Physical Description"), the available outline material consists of seven manuscript pages from three different drafts. Five of these pages are from draft C, and one page each is from drafts A and B. Together they cover the full book and overlap such that for slightly over half the chapters, two different drafts are available (See chart on page 26).

The transcript[1] that follows presents the final form of C, the latest and most complete of the three outlines. Clarifying text from previous drafts is included in {curly braces}, as Rowling would sometimes leave things out when rewriting, without intending to discard them. These are placed where relevant in the final transcript, regardless of where they appeared in the earlier drafts. Some earlier readings which *do* seem to have been discarded are given at the end.

In this transcript, Rowling's grid outline is presented linearly chapter by chapter, and her shorthand and abbreviations have been expanded. Column headings and some of the punctuation have been standardized. Bracketed words are inserted editorially [for flow]. Bracketed small caps words beginning with a question mark indicate [?UNCERTAIN] manuscript readings.

[1] See the bibliography on page 196 for where to find the original scans.

Chapter 1 – August – Dudley Demented

Plot	Harry desperate for information – contact – letters circumspect – desperate to rejoin [the] Weasleys – listening to news – Dudley showdown – meets Dementor – Mrs. Figg
Prophecy [1-3]	Voldemort plotting but badly informed – thinks anyone can take – Lucius Malfoy and Macnair casing joint
Hagrid/Grawp	Still with giants

Chapter 2 – August – A Peck of Owls

Plot	Confused letters from Ministry – Harry to bed very worried – newspapers (Daily Prophets) – 'Missy' Slipkiss
Snape/Dad[2]	Mention of Snape obliquely by Aunt Petunia
Hagrid/Grawp	Still with giants

Chapter 3 – August – The Auror's Guard

Plot	Moody, Tonks, and Lupin turn up to take Harry to Grimmauld [Place]. Finish [chapter] on entry to kitchen
Hagrid/Grawp	Still with giants

Chapter 4 – August – 12. Grimmauld Place

Plot	Dinner and masses of information. – Sirius explains Fudge's standpoint. – Ginny cheeky and funny – Mrs. Weasley worried – Percy – Fred and George planning – announce rental of small room in Diagon Alley – 'Missy' Slipkiss – George and V.[3] – House-elf and Hermione?
Prophecy	Lucius Malfoy to put Bode or anyone from Department of Mysteries under Imperius if get chance
Cho/Ginny	See plot
DA[4]	Meet for first time – explicit aims

---

[2] This heading is written variously in the manuscript as "Harry/Dad/Snape", "Harry/Snape/father", "Snape/Harry/father", and "Snape/Harry/Father".

[3] It is unclear who V. could be referring to. Perhaps Verity, who appears in the sixth book, but she is mentioned nowhere else in this outline.

[4] Note that Dumbledore's Army here refers to Dumbledore's resistance group, while Order of the Phoenix refers to Harry's clandestine Defense Against the Dark Arts club.

Snape/Dad	Snape not present – hint why
Hagrid/Grawp	Still with giants

Chapter 5 – August – The Ministry of Magic

Plot	Interrogation – Mrs. Figg witness – Dumbledore too – See entrance [to] Department of Mysteries – Percy
Prophecy	Lucius Malfoy hanging around Ministry on excellent terms with Fudge (puts Bode under)
DA	Still around
Hagrid/Grawp	Still with giants

Chapter 6 – August – Mrs. Weasley's Worst Fears

Plot	The clock – Mrs. Weasley's premonitions of doom – Percy etc. – more info and discussion – Ron and Hermione prefects – 'Missy' Slipkiss? – House-elf and Hermione?
Prophecy	Bode is under Imperius and under orders to proceed very cautiously
Cho/Ginny	Ginny here – Ginny / Hermione / Tonks
DA	around – Sirius farewell until Christmas
Hagrid/Grawp	Still with giants

Chapter 7 – September – Night Mares

Plot	Journey to Hogwarts – Cho on train – effort to speak to Harry while some others giving wide berth – arrival and see Thestral Horses – Grubbly Plank greets – up to castle for Sorting – no Hagrid – Sorting hat sings lament? about sad future and history being made again? Malfoy here? Professor Umbridge on train? [?COMING] here?
Prophecy	Bode knows on some level he can't do it
Cho/Ginny	Cho speaks [to Harry] – some others are shunning
Hagrid/Grawp [7-9]	Hagrid still with giants

Chapter 8 – September – Danger and Denial

Plot	Feast – Professor Umbridge introduced – her speech – Dumbledore's contrasting speech – Hermione and Ron given prefect bathroom keys and privileges [keys: C9 > C8]

Prophecy [8-9]	Voldemort impatiently awaits Bode's theft but it is very difficult (Harry hints? Confused visions?)

Chapter 9 – September – Joyce Umbridge

Plot	Exam emphasis – McGonagall first – prefect conversation – promise of careers guidance to whole class – first Umbridge lesson – Grubbly Plank substituting Hagrid – Snape? Potions?
DA	Can write in guarded way – Harry, Ron, and Hermione write and ask why no Hagrid

Chapter 10 – September / October – Blackout

Plot	Weekend – careers pamphlets – starting to get annoyed with Umbridge – Quidditch practice – Umbridge skulking – scar – Dumbledore – Snape lessons set up.
Prophecy	Bode hurt – "elementary mistake" – Harry sees Voldemort's subsequent fury
Cho/Ginny	Cho very attracted by scar – morbid – Ginny practical
DA	Bill says Madame Maxime was back for start of term

Chapter 11 – October – (Closed Mind)

Plot	Trelawney – Umbridge meddles – Snape lesson. Lights in Hagrid's hut. Harry and co go see – giants and general background – Hagrid badly injured – Umbridge complaint that they went
Prophecy	Voldemort plotting – can't make fresh attempt too soon, suspicion. Harry reads of Bode's "elementary mistake" – connects with Voldemort's fury – all tallies. Dumbledore's Army hanging around him – but thinks Bode was attacked
DA	writing in guarded fashion
Snape/Dad	Snape and Harry first lesson
Hagrid/Grawp	Hagrid returns badly injured with Grawp

Chapter 12 – October – Offense Against The Dark Arts

Plot	Care of Magical Creatures lesson [is] first [?FINAL THAT] Umbridge is [?GUNNING] – Gigantic row with Umbridge about teaching methods and Hagrid. Umbridge

	[?WARDEN] to Dumbledore. Dumbledore / Umbridge conversation? Order of the Phoenix idea.
Prophecy	Voldemort concocting new plan – still doesn't realize Harry and he have two-way connection
Cho/Ginny	Cho still more attracted but in morbid way. Contrast Ginny,
OP	Idea for Order of the Phoenix
Snape/Dad	Snape lessons continue
Hagrid/Grawp	Mysterious injuries continue

Chapter 13 – October – Plots and Resistance

Plot	Harry skips Snape lesson to go to Hogsmeade – {Harry, Ron, and Hermione meet Lupin and Tonks – can't talk,} Umbridge tailing – pass note. Harry, Ron, and Hermione recruiting for Order of the Phoenix – Hagrid fresh injuries – Hermione wants to incorporate SPEW in Order of the Phoenix – Daily Prophet story about Dumbledore's Army
Prophecy	Harry sees Hall of Prophecy [for] first time. Not sinister – beautiful.
Cho/Ginny	Cho {in Hogsmeade –} wants to join Order of the Phoenix
DA	Tonks and Lupin
OP	Recruiting
Snape/Dad	Harry skips {lesson to recruit for Order of the Phoenix} – Snape furious
Hagrid/Grawp	New injuries – covered in blood {stains} but Hermione reckons feeding – not his own blood – {"he's feeding something – that's not his blood"}

Chapter 14 – November – Dobby Finds

Plot	Umbridge now reading mail – Hedwig attacks – very bad Snape lesson – Harry can't do it (skipped last) – first meeting {of the Order of the Phoenix} – named
Prophecy	Voldemort still plotting – can't fathom what went wrong with Bode – decides to send Nagini on reconnaissance
Cho/Ginny	Cho and Ginny both present
DA	Umbridge intercepting mail
OP	First meeting
Snape/Dad	Snape lesson?

Hagrid/Grawp	Hagrid still being injured

Chapter 15 – November – The Dirtiest Tackle

Plot	Quidditch versus Malfoy – Harry suspended following foul – {attack on Malfoy after} Cedric taunt – firehead[5] with Sirius? – {that night,} can't sleep {following match} – restless – Umbridge – Malfoy – Cho – {concerns about scar –} finally falls asleep – sees Nagini attack Mr. Weasley
Prophecy	Nagini attacks Mr. Weasley. Voldemort sees Harry waking and shouting – realizes may be connected
Cho/Ginny	Cho adoring of Harry's tackle? – now madly in love – Ginny pleased ish
DA	{They can use} Firehead?
Hagrid/Grawp	Hagrid's lessons falling apart

Chapter 16 – real end November – Black Marks

Plot	Weasley kids hear of father. 'Missy' Slipkiss reaction to Mr Weasley's injury. Gryffindors angry at Harry - some torn. Fred and George action? Hermione contacts Rita. Order of the Phoenix meeting. Snape lesson. {Overview into Christmas.}
Prophecy	Voldemort has explanation of Bode – Nagini {got in,} saw warning that only those concerned in the prophecy can touch it.
Cho/Ginny	Cho, hearing when Harry fouled, madly in love. Kiss? Ginny worried about Dad.
DA	firehead about Arthur?
OP	{reactions – another} meeting {overview?}
Snape/Dad	Snape lesson very very bad – Harry saw snake / not working hard enough
Hagrid/Grawp	Hagrid in bad way – {still getting injuries} – Umbridge [?GUNNING]

Chapter 17 – December – Rita Returns

Plot	Hogsmeade - Christmas shopping – {they} meet Rita

[5] Firehead refers to floo communication. This never has an actual name in the books.

Prophecy Rita information – 'Missy' Slipkiss bargain struck
Cho/Ginny Harry now avoiding Cho a bit. Ginny and someone else? Seamus? met at Order of the Phoenix?
OP Order of the Phoenix
Hagrid/Grawp Hagrid [in] hospital wing. Grubbly Plank back
[17-18]

Chapter 18 – December – St. Mungo's Hospital for Magical Maladies and Injuries
Plot {St. Mungo's visit Christmas time –} See Lockhart – See Neville – See Bode {(Macnair visiting)} – See Arthur
Prophecy Voldemort now playing harry very subtly. Sees Hall of Prophecies again. Scar hurting only very slightly. {Could} see own name?
Cho/Ginny Ginny and Dad
DA around – Moody and eye?

Chapter 19 – December – (Xmas)
Prophecy Bode dead. Hall of Prophecy again
Cho/Ginny Hermione/Krum – Ginny and ?Seamus – {Ron [?SURLY NEGS]}
DA {Sirius here –} Big reunion

Chapter 20 – January – Extended Powers of Joyce Umbridge
Plot Harry misses match versus Hufflepuff – Order of the Phoenix now suspected by Umbridge – why weren't they all at match, might say students organizations specifically banned – Snape lesson
Prophecy [20-23] Harry learning – fighting increasingly strong visions but natural curiosity militating against – echo of patronus
Cho/Ginny Cho and Harry back on (ish)
OP {Order of the Phoenix} Big meeting
Snape/Dad Snape lesson overview? {Harry can mention Hall of Prophecy – Snape going ape at Harry because he can't do it}
Hagrid/Grawp Hagrid out of hospital [wing] {now} going purposely into forest armed with spikes etc

Chapter 21 – February – (Valentine's Day)

Plot	Date with Cho in Hogsmeade – thoroughly depressing – row – Cho in tears – Harry joins Hermione and Ron, depressed, at Rita meeting – Rita itching for details of Harry's personal life – back in time to see Trelawny ousted – dusk – Firenze replaces {in} nick of time. {"Didn't see that coming, did she?"}
Cho/Ginny	{very} miserable Valentine date {with Cho} – row
Snape/Dad	keep in view
Hagrid/Grawp	Hagrid cooking things up still

Chapter 22 – February – Cousin Grawp

Plot	Umbridge persecuting Hagrid. Firenze teaching prophecies and prophets – Harry, Ron, and Hermione go to have stiff discussion with Hagrid – meet Grawp – nightmare waiting to happen.
Cho/Ginny	Ginny great – Cho wants back {with Harry – another row} – Harry can't take
OP	Order of the Phoenix overview
Snape/Dad	keep in view
Hagrid/Grawp	They meet Grawp

Chapter 23 – March – Treason

Plot	Easter – discovery of Order of the Phoenix – Dumbledore takes the rap – "Then to Azkaban I must surely go. I trust I am allowed a toothbrush?" – Azkaban – He won't fight because Tonks is here and if she supports he'll blow Dumbledore's Army
DA	firehead – got to keep Lupin and Sirius going – BIG reaction here
Hagrid/Grawp	Hagrid clinging onto job by skin of teeth {refusing to abandon Grawp}

Chapter 24 – April – Careers Guidance

Plot	Careers consultation – Auror – Order of [the] Phoenix meeting {continues} – Ginny, Fred, and George extremely defiant to Umbridge – {Ginny} daubs {on the} wall {in temper} – Rita comes out for Harry in "The Questioner"

Prophecy	getting better
Cho/Ginny	Harry back with Cho at meeting – Dumbledore leaving has reconciled [them]
OP	{meeting – things hotting up with Fred and George}
Snape/Dad	overview – {Snape grudgingly approves ish} mention of progress

Chapter 25 – April – James Potter's Worst Hour

Plot	Snape snaping that it's about time Harry got it – putting him down etc – Harry sees Snape's worst day in Pensieve – Snape won't teach any more.
Prophecy	Harry now at Voldemort's mercy
Cho/Ginny	Ginny recipient of confidences
OP [25-26]	keep in view – meetings in corridors etc. [?GIVE] reaction to Fred and George going
Snape/Dad	See PLOT
Hagrid/Grawp	Hagrid and Grawp continue (unseen) – Hagrid won't give up on Grawp

Chapter 26 – April – Umbridge Ascendent

Plot	Hagrid sacked – misses lesson {Grubby Plank back again} – Harry sees Lupin/Sirius in fire – long discussion about his father. 'That's what Ginny said' – See Snape – Fred and George expelled
Prophecy	still fighting
Cho/Ginny	Cho not happy
Snape/Dad	Sirius furious with Snape

Chapter 27 – May – Azkaban Breakout

Plot	Quidditch – Fred and George gone Gryffindor flattened – Azkaban breakout – Rita
Prophecy [27-28]	Now like speeded up film[, Harry] sees Hall of Prophecies, where it is, close up on name, hour to set in – Voldemort has decided to go for it – breakout from Azkaban – unfortunately for him, Dumbledore[6] goes too, in hot pursuit – distract Aurors. Draw them away from

---

[6] Abbreviated as "D". Could also perhaps be "dementors".

	Ministry – have Harry clear – new vision of ?[7] dying in Hall of Prophecies
Cho/Ginny	Cho breaks it off

Chapter 28 – June – Thestral Horses

Plot	{end exam –} Voldemort breaks through – {Harry sets off – Thestral} horses and Neville and Ginny {Nightmarish flight pursued by Dementors}

Chapter 29 – June – Department of Mysteries

Plot	{Arrival at Ministry – Invisibility cloak on – Department of Mysteries (they fight way in) –} Entrance – death {room} – love {room seen} – {Into} Hall of Prophecies – no dying (?) but his name on Prophecy – {Harry} grabs {prophecy} – arrival of Death Eaters
Prophecy	DOESN'T REALISE UNTIL THERE THAT THE HALL CONTAINS PROPHECIES

Chapter 30 – June – Battle Death Eaters

Plot	{Battle Death Eaters –} arrival of Sirius and Co (alerted by Snape) – {Harry runs for it with prophecy but Sirius is in trouble – goes back –} Harry chucks {away the} prophecy – Sirius {chooses death rather than the Dementor – snake there – Voldemort comes}
Chapter[8]	{Hermione and Ron pull Harry back from death – now Voldemort, enraged. Furious, goes for Harry – Ministry wizards coming – Dumbledore – Voldemort throws Crabbe in front of himself – gone}
Chapter	{Back [at] Hogwarts – fall out – full explanations from Dumbledore – letter – prophecy – Neville etc.}
Chapter	{Journey home – <u>What else is Voldemort up to?</u>}

---

[7] The name of who Harry thought was dying is written as a '?', here and in chapter 29.

[8] C ends here. These next three entries are taken entirely from A, which has different chapter numbers and no chapter names.

Discarded text from earlier outline drafts

(10) end of term > start of term
(13) leak to Daily Prophet that Dumbledore is wanting to train army > Daily Prophet story about DA
(13) sees Cedric > sees Hall of P., etc.
(14) The Order of the Phoenix > Dobby finds
(14) Voldemort still formulating his plans. None of his Death Eaters able to get in and Polyjuice worthless. Department of Mysteries too well guarded. > Vol. still plotting, etc
(14) now censoring the mail > now reading mail > intercepting mail
(14) Harry still skipping Snape – not going > Snape lesson?
(16) Cho > Rita Returns > Hall of Prophecies > Black Marks
(16) Row about skipping Snape lessons – Harry really in doghouse – he angry > Snape lesson
(16) has confirmation of Bode's story > has explanation of Bode
(16) Ron and rest of Weasleys called in to be told of father's injury > firehead about Arthur?
(16) Row about Harry not going > Snape lesson very very bad
(18) leg > eye
(18) Now Voldemort is actively trying to get Harry to Hall of Prophecies – very vivid > Voldemort now playing harry very subtly, etc.
(19) Xmas > Grimmauld Place > Christmas > (Xmas)
(19) boyfriend > ?Seamus
(20) Elvira > Joyce
(20) now being hunted by Umbridge > now suspected by Umbridge
(20) but not very successfully > but natural curiosity overcoming > but natural curiosity militating against
(21) Rita reports back on Bode etc. > Rita itching for details of Harry's personal life
(21) they could row > row
(22) now really going for Hagrid. > persecuting Hagrid.
(22) go to warn Hagrid > go to have stiff discussion with Hagrid
(22) see Grawp > meet Grawp
(24) Harry starting to get it – blocking out > Harry starting to get it now. > getting better
(25) worst memory > worst day
(26) May > April; Exent Weasleys > Umbridge Ascendent
(27) final vision > new vision
(28) Exams > Thestral Horses
(30) until arrival of > arrival of
(30) but Sirius chooses death > Sirius chooses death > Sirius dies
(32) explanations from Dumbledore > fall out – full explanations from Dumbledore

Moved content

Prefect bathroom keys: C9 > C8
Daily Prophet story: C12 > C13
Rita Returns: B16 > B17 > C17
See own name: B18 > C18 > C27
Cho wants back: B23 > C22
Hagrid clinging onto job: B24 > C23
getting better: B23 > B24 > C24
mention progress: B23 > B24 > C24
Hagrid sacked: C24 > C23 > C26
Sirius furious with Snape: C25 > C26
A23 > C25; A24 > C26-C27;
A25-27 > C28-C29; A28-29 > C30

Appendix B: Chapter Correspondence

Outline Chapters	Published Chapters
1. Dudley Demented	1. Dudley Demented
2. A Peck of Owls	2. A Peck of Owls
3. The Auror's Guard	3. The Advance Guard
4. 12. Grimmauld Place	4. Number Twelve Grimmauld Place 5. The Order of the Phoenix
5. The Ministry of Magic	7. The Ministry of Magic 8. The Hearing
6. Mrs. Weasley's Worst Fears	9. The Woes of Mrs Weasley
7. Night Mares	10. Luna Lovegood
8. Danger and Denial	11. The Sorting Hat's New Song
9. Joyce Umbridge	12. Professor Umbridge
10. Blackout	13. Detention with Dolores
11. Closed Mind	15. The Hogwarts High Inquisitor 20. Hagrid's Tale 24. Occlumency
12. Offense Against The Dark Arts	15. The Hogwarts High Inquisitor 21. The Eye of the Snake
13. Plots and Resistance	16. In the Hog's Head

~~14. The Order of the Phoenix~~ 14. Dobby finds	18. Dumbledore's Army
15. The Dirtiest Tackle	19. The Lion and the Serpent 21. The Eye of the Snake
16. Black Marks	14. Percy and Padfoot
17. Rita Returns	
18. St. Mungo's Hospital for Magical Maladies and Injuries	22. St. Mungo's Hospital for Magical Maladies and Injuries 23. Christmas on the Closed Ward
~~19. Grimmauld Place~~ 19. Xmas	22. St. Mungo's Hospital for Magical Maladies and Injuries
20. Extended Powers of Joyce Umbridge	17. Educational Decree Number Twenty-Four
21. Valentine's Day	25. The Beetle at Bay 26. Seen and Unforseen
22. Cousin Grawp	27. The Centaur and the Sneak 30. Grawp
23. Treason	27. The Centaur and the Sneak
24. Careers Guidance	26. Seen and Unforseen 29. Career Advice
25. James Potter's Worst Hour	28. Snape's Worst Memory 29. Career Advice
~~26. Exent Weasleys~~ 26. Umbridge Ascendent	29. Career Advice
27. Azkaban Breakout	30. Grawp
~~28. Exams~~ 28. Thestral Horses	31. O.W.L.S. 33. Fight and Flight 34. The Department of Mysteries
29. Department of Mysteries	34. The Department of Mysteries
30. Battle Death Eaters	35. Beyond the Veil

Appendix C: Dates of the Outline

Outline	Published Book
August	
Dementor attack	Dementor attack
Grimmauld Place	Grimmauld Place
Ministry hearing	Ministry hearing
Journey to Hogwarts	Journey to Hogwarts
September	
Term Begins	Term Begins
	Idea for DA
October	
Occlumency starts	First DA Meeting
Hagrid returns	Umbridge bans student orgs
Idea for OP	Hedwig attacked
First OP Meeting	
November	
Hedwig attacked	Hagrid returns
Harry/Cho kiss	
Mr. Weasley attacked	
Voldemort learns why Bode couldn't take prophecy	
December	
Meet with Rita in Hogsmeade	Harry/Cho kiss
Leave to Grimmauld Place	Mr. Weasley attacked
St Mungos visit	Leave to Grimmauld Place
Bode killed	St Mungos visits

January	
Umbridge bans student orgs	Occlumency starts Azkaban breakout Bode killed
February	
Cho date / Rita interview Trelawney ousted Meet Grawp	Cho date / Rita interview Rita interview published Voldemort learns why Bode couldn't take prophecy
March	
OP discovered Dumbledore arrested	Trelawney ousted
April	
Career Guidance Rita interview published Snape's worst memory Hagrid sacked Fred and George expelled	DA discovered Dumbledore sacked Career Guidance Fred and George leave
May	
Lose Quidditch Final Azkaban breakout	Win Quidditch Final Meet Grawp
June	
Vision of ? dying Exams Thestrals Ministry battle Journey home	O.W.L.s Hagrid sacked Vision of Sirius tortured Thestrals Ministry battle Journey home

Bibliography

This bibliography will be split into sections. The first part is a very detailed publication history of the *Order of the Phoenix* outline itself. This manuscript is the central focus of this collection, and its publication history is rather complicated. It is therefore described here in a fuller and more technical form than usual, noting what the various available sources are, and noting which of the manuscript pages were displayed or reproduced in each source.[1]

The second part will be a complete list of all primary J.K. Rowling sources referenced in this volume, but including more detail, and including weblinks where appropriate.

This will be followed by a list of all referenced *Harry Potter* secondary sources, and then by a list of all other referenced sources.

[1] There are seven published pages from the outline, which can be noted by their manuscript version and chapter numbers. One of the pages has been published in two distinct scans, leading to a total of eight available image scans: "A23-34", "B13-24a", "B13-24b", "C1-6", "C7-12", "C13-18", "C19-24", "C25-30".

The Order of the Phoenix Outline

★ Museum Exhibitions[2]

Harry Potter: A History of Magic, 20 Oct. 2017–28 Feb. 2018, British Library

Harry Potter: A History of Magic, 5 Oct. 2018–27 Jan. 2019, NY Historical Society

Harry Potter to Mahō no Rekishi, 11 Sep. 2021–7 Nov. 2021, Hyogo Prefectural Museum of Art

Harry Potter to Mahō no Rekishi, 18 Dec. 2021 – 27 Mar. 2022, Tokyo Station Gallery

★ Documentaries

Harry Potter: A History of Magic. BBC Two, 28 Oct. 2017, 52:14–52:16. All seven pages briefly appear on screen, none are readable.

★ Print Publications[3]

Horwitz, Stuart. *Book Architecture: How to Plot and Outline Without Using a Formula*. 15 May 2015, p. 75. ISBN 9780986420405. Includes a 3.2" reproduction and approximate transcript of "B13-24a", with some commentary by Horwitz and Cary Plocher.

"Planning the Order of the Phoenix". *Harry Potter: A History of Magic*, UK ed., Bloomsbury, 20 Oct. 2017, pp. 240-241. ISBN 9781408890769. Eight known reissues, including translations

---

[2] All seven known pages from the outline were prominently displayed at each of the four exhibitions.

[3] The dimensions given for each print or digital reproduction refers to the height of the image in inches or pixels.

into German, Japanese, French, Turkish, Hungarian, Russian, and Ukrainian. Includes a 5" reproduction of "B13-24b" and 2.6" reproductions of the other six pages.

"Planning the Order of the Phoenix". *Harry Potter: A Journey Through A History of Magic*, Bloomsbury, 20 Oct. 2017, pp. 128-29. ISBN 9781408890776. Seventeen known reissues, including translations into Italian, Japanese, French, Spanish, Polish, Czech, Serbian, Turkish, Vietnamese, Swedish, Danish, Hungarian, Thai, Chinese, and Finnish. Includes a 5.9" reproduction of "B13-24b", a 5.8" reproduction of "C1-6", and 1.4" reproductions of the other five pages.

"Planning the Order of the Phoenix". *Harry Potter: A History of Magic*, US ed., Arthur A. Levine Books, 9 Oct. 2018, pp. 240-45. ISBN 9781338311501. Includes a 4.4" reproduction of "B13-24b" and 4.5" reproductions of the other six pages. For most of the pages this is the highest quality print reproduction available.

"Fushichōnokishidan" no kōsō (『不死鳥の騎士団』の構想)". *Harry Potter: to Mahō no Rekishi (ハリー・ポッターと魔法の歴史)*, Seizansha, 18 Mar. 2022, pp. 246-47. ISBN 9784863896376. Includes a 5" reproduction of "B13-24b" and 2.6" reproductions of the other six pages.

★ Digital Publications

"Revision of the plan of 'Order of the Phoenix'". *J.K. Rowling Official Site*, www.jkrowling.com, Available 9 Mar. 2006–23 Feb. 2012. 1500px reproduction of "B13-24a". Archived on *The Rowling* Library, www.therowlinglibrary.com/jkrowling.com. To access, click the eyeglasses and wait for peeves, then click the hairbrush and draw a lighting bolt.

"Planning the Order of the Phoenix". *Harry Potter: A History of Magic*, UK ed., E-book ed., Pottermore Publishing, 20 Oct. 2017, pp. 304-307. ISBN 9781781109472. Includes 1000px reproductions of "B13-24b" and the other six pages. These images are also less compressed than in the other two eBooks.

"Planning the Order of the Phoenix". *Harry Potter: A Journey Through A History of Magic*, E-book ed., Pottermore Publishing, 20 Oct. 2017, pp. 190-91. ISBN 9781781109502. Includes 800px reproductions of "B13-24b" and "C1-6", and 250px reproductions of the other five pages.

"Planning the Order of the Phoenix". *Harry Potter: A History of Magic*, US ed., E-book ed., Pottermore Publishing, 9 Oct. 2018, pp. 346-351. ISBN 9781781102596. Includes a 600px reproduction of "B13-24b", and 650px reproductions of the other six pages.

J.K. Rowling Sources

★ Books

Fantastic Beasts and Where to Find Them. Bloomsbury, 2001.

Harry Potter and the Chamber of Secrets. Bloomsbury, 1998.

Harry Potter and the Deathly Hallows. Bloomsbury, 2007.

Harry Potter and the Goblet of Fire. Bloomsbury, 2000.

Harry Potter and the Half Blood Prince. Bloomsbury, 2005.

Harry Potter and the Order of the Phoenix. Bloomsbury, 2003.

Harry Potter and the Philosopher's Stone. Bloomsbury, 1997.

Harry Potter and the Prisoner of Azkaban. Bloomsbury, 1999.

[*Published as* Robert Galbraith]. *The Cuckoo's Calling*. Sphere, 2013.

[*Published as* Robert Galbraith]. *Lethal White*. Sphere, 2018.

[*Published as* Robert Galbraith]. *Troubled Blood*. Sphere, 2020.

Quidditch through the Ages. Bloomsbury, 2001.

★ Interviews

Interview. *Harry Potter and Me*. BBC, 28 Dec. 2001. Transcript available on *Accio-Quote*, www.accio-quote.org/articles/2001/1201-bbc-hpandme.htm. Recording available on *YouTube*, www.youtube.com/watch?v=SrJiAG8GmnQ.

Interview. "How I Write." *The Sunday Times*, 5 May 2024, *Culture* magazine, pp. 4–5. Available on *The Times*, www.thetimes.com/culture/books/article/jk-rowling-books-writing-harry-potter-strike-bdg7gtg5q. Recording available on *YouTube*, www.youtube.com/watch?v=3uLa3WKXwLg.

Interview. "J.K. Rowling Open Book Tour." Carnegie Hall, New York, 19 Oct. 2007. Transcript available on *The Leaky Cauldron*, www.the-leaky-cauldron.org/2007/10/20/j-k-rowling-at-carnegie-hall-reveals-dumbledore-is-gay-neville-marries-hannah-abbott-and-scores-more.

Interview. "By the Book: J.K. Rowling." *The New York Times*, 14 Oct. 2012, p. BR8. *Sunday Book Review*. Available on *The New York Times*, www.nytimes.com/2012/10/14/books/review/j-k-rowling-by-the-book.html.

Interview by Adeel Amini. *The Student* [Edinburgh], 4 March 2008. Transcript available on *The Rowling Library*, www.therowlinglibrary.com/2024/08/28/the-adeel-amini-interview-with-j-k-rowling-2008.

Interview by Ann Treneman. "Harry and Me" *The Times* [London], 30 June 2000, Times2 supp., pp. 3-7. Available on *Accio-Quote*, www.accio-quote.org/articles/2000/0600-times-treneman.html.

Interview by Billy DiMichele. *Harry Potter: Beyond the Page: A Virtual Author Visit with J.K. Rowling*. Scholastic, Harry Potter Reading Club, 11 Oct. 2012. Transcript available on *Snitch Seeker*, www.snitchseeker.com/harry-potter-news/jk-rowling-full-harry-potter-reading-club-webchat-discussion-transcript-now-available-91349. Recording available on *YouTube*, www.youtube.com/watch?v=aA_QYZBWQ88.

Interview by Charlie Rose. *Charlie Rose*, 19 Oct. 2012. Available at charlierose.com/episodes/17140.

Interview by Christopher Lydon. *The Connection*. WBUR, 12 Oct. 1999. Transcript available on *Accio-Quote*, www.accio-quote.org/articles/1999/1099-connectiontransc2.htm. Recording available on *YouTube*, www.youtube.com/watch?v=QH89ZeIeNfA.

Interview by Emerson Spartz and Melissa Anelli. "The MuggleNet and Leaky Cauldron Interview with Joanne Kathleen Rowling." *MuggleNet*, 16 July 2005, www.mugglenet.com/2005/07/emerson-spartz-and-melissa-anelli-the-mugglenet-and-leaky-cauldron-interview-joanne-kathleen-rowling.

Interview by Evan Solomon. *Hot Type*. CBC Newsworld, 13 July 2000. Transcript available on *Accio-Quote*, www.accio-quote.org/articles/2000/0700-hottype-solomon.htm. Recording available on *YouTube*, www.youtube.com/watch?v=XbsqZJ9rMD0.

Interview by Geordie Greig. "There would be so much to tell her..." *Tatler Magazine*, February 2006, pp. 128–35. Available on *Accio-Quote*, www.accio-quote.org/articles/2006/0110-tatler-grieg.html.

Interview by Ian Parker. "Mugglemarch: J.K. Rowling writes a realist novel for adults." *The New Yorker*, 1 October 2012, pp. 52–63. Available on *The New Yorker*, www.newyorker.com/magazine/2012/10/01/mugglemarch.

Interview by Jeremy Paxman. *BBC Newsnight*, BBC Two, 19 June 2003. Transcript available on *Accio-Quote*, www.accio-quote.org/articles/2003/0619-bbcnews-paxman.htm. Recording available on *YouTube*, www.youtube.com/watch?v=G2tcbFF99Yg.

Interview by Kaitlin Bolger and J.T. Sprague. *Newsday*, 18 Jan. 2001. Available on *Chron*, www.chron.com/culture/main/article/interview-j-k-rowling-answers-a-few-kid-2010938.php

Interview by Katie Couric. *Today Show*. NBC, 20 Oct. 2000. Transcript available on *Accio-Quote*, www.accio-quote.org/articles/2000/1000-nbc-couric.htm.

Interview by Larry King. "J.K. Rowling Discusses the Surprising Success of 'Harry Potter.'" *Larry King Live*. CNN, 20 Oct. 2000. Transcript available on *Accio-Quote*, www.accio-quote.org/articles/2000/1000-cnn-larryking.htm.

Interview by Lesley Stahl. *60 Minutes*, CBS, 12 Sept. 1999. Bonus segment "Plotting Potter", released online 25 Oct. 2006. Recording available on *YouTube*, www.youtube.com/watch?v=V_m0V1OLaKo.

Interview by Lizo Mzimba. "JK Rowling talks about Book Four." *CBBC Newsround*, 8 July 2000. Transcript available on *Accio-Quote*, www.accio-quote.org/articles/2000/0700-cbbc-mzimba.htm.

Interview by Lizo Mzimba. "Newsround talks exclusively to J.K. Rowling," *CBBC Newsround*, 19 Sept. 2002. Transcript available on *Accio-Quote*, www.accio-quote.org/articles/2002/0902-newsround-mzimba.html.

Interview by Meredith Vieira. "JK Rowling One-On-One" *Today Show*, NBC, 27 July 2007. Transcript available on *Accio-Quote*, www.accio-quote.org/articles/2007/0726-today-vieira2.html.

Interview by Simon Armitage. *The Poet Laureate Has Gone to His Shed*, extended version, *BBC Sounds*, www.bbc.co.uk/sounds/play/m000y5th. Originally broadcast on *BBC Radio 4*, 24 July 2021. Extended version released 24 July 2021. Also available on *YouTube*, www.youtube.com/watch?v=LUHmcVl5qok.

Interview by Stephen Fry. "Launch Day interview aboard the Hogwarts Express." *Bloomsbury Press*, 8 July 2000. Transcript available on *Accio-Quote*, www.accio-quote.org/articles/2000/0700-bloomsbury-fry.html. Recording available on *YouTube*, www.youtube.com/watch?v=nDbqqfOyarI.

Interview by Stephen Fry. *Fantastic Beasts: A Natural History. BBC One*, 27 Feb. 2022. Recording available on *YouTube*, www.youtube.com/watch?v=HIcQrUXwxO0.

Interview by Wilma de Rek. *de Volkskrant*. 17 Nov. 2007, www.volkskrant.nl/cultuur-media/j-k-rowling~b25d90dd. Dutch. English translation available on *The Leaky Cauldron*, www.the-leaky-cauldron.org/2007/11/19/new-interview-with-j-k-rowling-for-release-of-dutch-edition-of-deathly-hallows.

Webchat with Barnes & Noble. *barnesandnoble.com*. 20 Oct. 2000. Transcript available on *Accio-Quote*, www.accio-quote.org/articles/2000/1000-livechat-barnesnoble.html.

★ Manuscripts

"Autograph Card Signed ('J.K. Rowling') Referring to the Forthcoming Book Harry Potter and the Order of the Phoenix." Partially reproduced in *English Literature, History, Private Press & Children's Books*, Sotheby's, 12 Dec. 2002, lot 517, p. 229. Also in *English Literature, History, Children's Books and Illustrations*, Sotheby's, 3-10 Dec. 2019, lot 244, p. 116.

"Chapter Six: The Journey from Platform Nine and Three Quarters." Handwritten manuscript draft. British Library, exhibited as part of *Writing Britain: Wastelands to Wonderlands*, 11 May–25 Sept. 2012.

"Chapter 7: The Sorting Hat." Handwritten manuscript outline. National Portrait Gallery, exhibited as part of *Beatrix Potter to Harry Potter: Portraits of Children's Writers*, 15 May–26 Aug. 2002.

Chapter outline for *The Cuckoo's Calling*. jkrowling.com, 20 Dec. 2016, www.jkrowling.com/wp-content/themes/jkrowling/assets/images/notebook.png.

Chapter outline for Harry Potter and the Goblet of Fire. Shown on *60 Minutes*, CBS, 12 Sept. 1999. Recording available on *YouTube*, www.youtube.com/watch?v=gjWABn5imBw.

Handwritten list of students in Harry's year. Shown on Harry Potter and Me. BBC, 28 Dec. 2001. Recording available on YouTube, www.youtube.com/watch?v=SrJiAG8GmnQ.

Handwritten lists of Hogwarts subjects and teachers. Originally published on *J.K. Rowling Official Site*, www.jkrowling.com, 9 Mar. 2006 and 31 Oct. 2007. Later featured in *Harry Potter: A History of Magic*, British Library, 2017. Printed in *Harry Potter: A History of Magic*, British Library, 2017, pp. 124-25. Available at artsandculture.google.com/asset/eAEbJC9YvFjySw.

★ Other J.K Rowling Writings

"*I plan a lot. This particular novel's plan comprises a vast, complicated, colour-coded table showing all the suspects, with blue ink for clues and red ink for red herrings.*" *X*, 30 Jan. 2018, x.com/jk_rowling/status/958382036556886016

"No Writer's Block." The Scotsman, 9 Aug. 2001, p.13, Letters to the Editor. Available on *Accio-Quote*, www.accio-quote.org/articles/2001/1001-scotsman-rowling.html.

"*These plans date from around 2001/2.*" Wall text for *Planning the Order of the Phoenix. Harry Potter: A History of Magic*, 20 Oct. 2017–28 Feb. 2018, British Library. Printed in *Harry Potter: A Journey Through a History of Magic*, British Library, 20 Oct. 2017, p. 128.

"Dolores Umbridge." *Pottermore*, 31 Oct. 2014, archived on *Wizarding World*, www.harrypotter.com/writing-by-jk-rowlin g/dolores-umbridge.

"Florean Fortescue." *Pottermore*, 5 Dec. 2014, archived on *Wizarding World*, www.harrypotter.com/writing-by-jk-rowlin g/florean-fortescue.

"Mafalda." *Extra Stuff, J.K. Rowling Official Site*, 15 May 2004. Archived on *The Rowling Library*, www.therowlinglibrary.com/jkrowling.com/textonly/en/extrastuff_view_id=3.html

"My Story." *J.K. Rowling's Stories*, 9 Sept. 2021, stories.jkrowling.co m/en-us/my-story.

"The Original Forty." *Pottermore*, 15 Aug. 2011, archived on *Wizarding World*, www.harrypotter.com/writing-by-jk-rowling/the-original-forty.

Harry Potter Secondary Sources

Anelli, Melissa. *Harry, a History*. Simon & Schuster, 2008.

Beckoff, Laurie. "It's All Fun and Games Until...: Leisurely and Competitive Pursuits in Harry Potter and Chivalric Romance." *Potterversity: Essays Exploring the World of Harry Potter*, edited by Kathryn McDaniel and Emily Strand, McFarland & Company, Inc., 2024, pp. 179-192.

Bracchi, Paul. "What Is JK Rowling's Obsession with Death? Author Reveals Her Dark Side and Why the Subject Helps Her Deal with Mortality." *Daily Mail*, 27 Sept. 2012, www.dailymail.co.uk/news/article-2209730/JK-Rowlings-release-novel-The-Casual-Vacancy-shrouded-secrecy.html.

ChicoStroke. "Harry and Voldemort are one and the same, because Voldemort did not die" *Harry Latino*, 2 Aug, 2004, web.archive.org/web/20040812100318/http://www.harrylatino.net/index.php?showtopic=23000

DarklzBlo. "What's your least favorite Harry Potter book from all 7 books?" *Reddit*, 30 Nov. 2023, www.reddit.com/r/harrypotter/comments/z8y8d1/whats_your_least_favorite_harry_potter_book_from.

Errington, Philip W. *J.K. Rowling: A Bibliography 1997-2013*. Bloomsbury Academic, 23 Apr. 2015, p. 274.

Fantastic Beasts: The Crimes of Grindelwald. Directed by David Yates, Warner Brother, 2018.

Fantastic Beasts: The Secrets of Dumbledore. Directed by David Yates, Warner Brothers., 2022.

Fransisca, Marcelina, and Jenny Mochtar. "The Role of Girls as Mothers in the Harry Potter Series." *k@ta*, vol. 19, no. 1, 2017, pp. 1-7.

Freeman, Louise M. "The Ghost of His Last Laugh: Evolving Humor in Harry Potter." *The Ivory Tower, Harry Potter and Beyond: More Essays on the Works of J.K. Rowling*, edited by Lana. A. Whited, University of Missouri Press, 2023, pp. 133-151.

———. "Harry Potter and the Diagnostic and Statistical Manual: Muggle Disorders in the Wizarding World." *Study & Scrutiny: Research on Young Adult Literature*, vol. 1, no. 1, 2015, pp. 156-214.

Granger, John. "The Adeel Amini – Jo Rowling Interview." *Hogwarts Professor*, 30 Mar. 2008, www.hogwartsprofessor.com/the-adeel-amini-jo-rowling-interview. Nota Bene, Feb. 2018.

———. *The Deathly Hallows Lectures: The Hogwarts Professor Explains Harry's Final Adventure.* Zossima Press, 2008.

———. Guest. "Harry Potter." *Beyond Belief*. BBC Radio 4, 23 Aug. 2021.

———. *Harry Potter as Ring Composition and Ring Cycle.* Lulu, 2010.

———. "How does 'Ring Composition' Work, Anyway?" *Hogwarts Professor*, 19 Nov. 2010, www.hogwartsprofessor.com/ring-composition-25-off-on-cyber-monday-how-does-ring-composition-work-anyway.

———. *The Hogwarts Saga as Ring Composition and Ring Cycle.* Unlocking Press, 2010.

———. "The Literary Alchemy of J.K. Rowling." *The Alchemical Harry Potter: Essays on Transfiguration in the Novels of J.K. Rowling*, edited by Anne J. Mamary, McFarland & Company, Inc., 2020, pp. 30–45.

———. "Ring Composition." *Hogwarts Professor*, 25 Dec. 2018, www.hogwartsprofessor.com/ring-composition.

Groves, Beatrice. "Hits-and-Misses, Folk Horror and Shakespearean Pastoral: Running Grave First Thoughts." *Hogwarts Professor*, 31 Oct. 2023, www.hogwartsprofessor.com/beatrice-groves-hits-and-misses-folk-horror-and-shakespearean-pastoral.

———. "'It's Just Like Waking Up, Right?': 'Crimes of Grindelwald', Kipling, and Shakespeare's Midsummer Dreaming." *MuggleNet*, 12 Nov. 2018, www.mugglenet.com/2018/11/its-just-like-waking-up-right-the-crimes-of-grindelwald-kipling-and-shakespeares-midsummer-dreaming.

———. *Literary Allusion in Harry Potter*. Routledge, 2017.

———. "The Phoenix and the Qilin in 'Secrets of Dumbledore': Fantastic Bestiaries and Where to Find Them – Part 3." *MuggleNet*, 7 Apr. 2022, www.mugglenet.com/2022/04/the-phoenix-and-the-qilin-in-secrets-of-dumbledore-fantastic-bestiaries-and-where-to-find-them-part-3.

———. "Shakespeare and *Harry Potter* – Part 1." *MuggleNet*, 28 June 2017, www.mugglenet.com/2017/06/literary-allusion-harry-potter-shakespeare-harry-potter-part-1.

———. "A Shakespearean Source for the Four-Point Character Conflict in *Harry Potter*?" *MuggleNet*, 23 Apr. 2018, www.mugglenet.com/2018/04/a-shakespearean-source-for-harry-potters-four-point-character-conflict.

Harry Potter and the Prisoner of Azkaban. Directed by Alfonso Cuarón, Warner Bros., 2004.

Haber, Dave. "Dumbledore Clues." *DumbledoreIsNotDead*, 19 July 2005, dumbledoreisnotdead.com/dumbledoreclues.

Harper, Caitlin Elizabeth. "Quidditch as Narrative Mirror in the Harry Potter Series." *The Ivory Tower, Harry Potter and Beyond: More Essays on the Works of J.K. Rowling*, edited by Lana A. Whited, University of Missouri Press, 2023, pp. 169-184.

Khaytman, Irvin. *Dumbledore*. Media Lab Books, 2021.

——— [hpboy13]. "The Missing Halloweens – Part 2: 'Order of the Phoenix'." *MuggleNet*, 21 Oct. 2022, www.mugglenet.com/2022/10/the-missing-halloweens-part-2-order-of-the-phoenix.

King, Stephen. "Potter Gold: Stephen King Takes a Shining to J.K. Rowling's Delightfully Dark *Harry Potter and the Order of the Phoenix*." *Entertainment Weekly*, no. 718, 11 July 2003, pp. 80–

81. Available at ew.com/books/2009/08/01/harry-potter-and-order-phoenix-4.

Lynch, Evanna. Foreword. *From the Wizarding Archive: Curated Writing from the World of Harry Potter*, by J.K. Rowling, Pottermore Publishing, 2024.

Markell, Kathryn A., and Marc A. Markell. *The Children Who Lived: Using Harry Potter and Other Fictional Characters to Help Grieving Children and Adolescents*. Routledge, 2008.

Neal, Connie. *The Gospel According to Harry Potter, Revised and Expanded Edition: The Spiritual Journey of the World's Greatest Seeker*. Westminster/John Knox Press, 2008.

Pasola, Kate. "The Integrity of Luna Lovegood: How J.K. Rowling Subverts the 'Magic Pixie Dream Girl' Trope." *Charming and Bewitching: Considering the Harry Potter Series*, edited by S.M. Alegre, Universitat Autonoma de Barcelona, 2014, pp. 153-161.

Provenzano, David, and Richard Heyman. "Harry Potter and the Resilience to Adversity." *The Psychology of Harry Potter: An Unauthorized Examination of the Boy Who Lived*, edited by Neil Mulholland, Smart Pop, 2006, pp. 105-199.

Roonil_Wazlib97. Comment on "In OOTP, Why It's So Important for Order to Prevent Voldemort from Getting the Prophecy?" by EitherPhase5676. *Reddit*, 28 Feb. 2023, www.reddit.com/r/harrypotter/comments/11e59g1/in_ootp_why_its_so_important_for_order_to_prevent/jaci6lv.

Sanna, Antonio. "'I Can Touch Him Now:' Harry Potter as a Gothic Narrative of Trauma and Homoerotic Sexual Abuse." *Literary Refractions*, vol. 5, no. 1, 2015, pp. 1-17.

Sinyor, Mark, et al. "The Boy Who Lived Well: Harry Potter as a Novel Tool for Teaching Cognitive-Behavioural Skills to Youth." *Journal of the American Academy of Child and Adolescent Psychiatry Connect*, vol. 4, no. 2, 2017, pp. 15-21.

Smith, Laura Lee. "Who Deserves the Truth? A Look at Veracity and Mendacity in Harry Potter." *Harry Potter for Nerds II: Essays for Fans, Academics, and Lit Geeks*, edited by Kathryn McDaniel and Travis Prinzi, Unlocking Press, 2015, pp. 271-291.

Spartz, Emerson, and Ben Schoen. *Harry Potter Should Have Died: Controversial Views from the #1 Fan Site*. Ulysses Press, 2009.

Spartz, Emerson, et al. *Mugglenet's What Will Happen in Harry Potter 7: Who Lives, Who Dies, Who Falls in Love, and How Will the Adventure Finally End*. Ulysses Press, 2006.

Strand, Emily. "The Second War Was Won on the Quidditch Pitch of Hogwarts." *Harry Potter for Nerds II: Essays for Fans, Academics, and Lit Geeks*, edited by Kathryn McDaniel and Travis Prinzi, Unlocking Press, 2015, pp. 115-138.

Tarantino, Patricio. *Secret History of the Wizarding Phenomenon: How the Harry Potter Books, Movies, Theme Parks, and More Came to Life*. TRL Books, 20 Sept. 2021.

Tonkin, Boyd. "The Boy Hero Becomes Dirty Harry in This Downbeat Read." Review of *Harry Potter and the Order of the Phoenix*, by J.K. Rowling. *The Independent*, no. 5204, 23 June 2003, p. 6. Available at www.independent.co.uk/arts-entertainment/books/reviews/harry-potter-and-the-order-of-the-phoenix-by-jk-rowling-109924.html.

Other Sources

Beauregard, David. "'The Mutual Flame of Love': Spiritual Marriage in Shakespeare's *The Phoenix and Turtle*." *Religion and the Arts*, vol. 15, 2011, pp. 131–47.

The Bible. King James Version, 1611.

Brody, Robert. *Mishna and Tosefta Studies*. Magnus Press, 2015.

Burrow, Colin. "I, Lowborn Cur" Review of *Literary Names: Personal Names in English Literature*, by Alastair Fowler. *London Review of Books*, vol. 34 no. 22, 22 November 2012, pp. 15–17.

Chapman, Tracy, and Terry Chi. "Perceived Social Support Mediates the Link Between Optimism and Active Coping." *Journal of Behavioral and Social Sciences*, vol. 4, no. 2, 2017, pp. 57-65.

Cohen, Walter. "The Phoenix and Turtle." *The Norton Shakespeare*, edited by Stephen Greenblatt et al., 3rd ed., W.W. Norton & Co., 2016, pp. 1973–75.

Cunningham, J. V. "'Essence' and the *Phoenix and Turtle*." *English Literary History*, vol. 4, 1952, pp. 265–76.

Cutsinger, James S. *The Form of Transformed Vision: Coleridge and the Knowledge of God*. Mercer University Press, 1988.

DeVellis, Robert F., Brenda M. DeVellis, and Charley McCauley. "Vicarious Acquisition of Learned Helplessness." *Journal of Personality and Social Psychology*, vol. 36, no. 8, 1978, pp. 894-899.

Douglas, Mary. *Thinking in Circles: An Essay on Ring Composition*. Yale University Press, 2007.

Eliade, Mircea. *The Myth of the Eternal Return: Or, Cosmos and History*. Princeton University Press, 1971.

———. *The Two and the One*. University of Chicago Press, 1979.

Fitzgerald, F. Scott. *The Last Tycoon*. Charles Scribner's Sons, 1941.

Ghbari, Thaer A., Jalal Kayed Damra, and Yahya H. Nassar. "The Effect of Learned Helplessness on Changing Goal Orientation Among Undergraduate Students." *Journal of Institutional Research in South East Asia*, vol. 12, no. 1, 2014, pp. 110-120.

Guénon, René. *The Symbolism of the Cross*. 1931. Sophia Perennis et Universalis, 2001.

Jones, Valerie. "The Phoenix and the Resurrection." *The Mark of the Beast: The Medieval Bestiary in Art, Life and Literature*, edited by Debra Hassig, Garland Publishing, 1999, pp. 99–116.

Kaufman, Joan, et al. "Social Supports and Serotonin Transporter Genes Moderate Depression in Maltreated Children." *Proceedings of the National Academy of Sciences*, vol. 101, no. 49, 2004, pp. 17136-17141.

Kim, H. Y., Huh, H. J. & Chase, J. H. (2015). Effects of religiosity and spirituality on the treatment response in patients with depressive disorders. Comprehensive Psychiatry 60, 26-34.

Maier, Steven F., and Martin E. P. Seligman. "Learned Helplessness at Fifty: Insights from Neuroscience." *Psychological Review*, vol. 123, no. 4, 2016, pp. 349-367.

Seligman, Martin. "Flourish: Positive Psychology and Positive Interventions." *The Tanner Lectures on Human Values*, edited by Mark Matheson, vol. 31, 2012, pp. 229-243. Delivered at The University of Michigan, 7 Oct. 2010.

———. "Learned Helplessness." *Annual Review of Medicine*, vol. 23, no. 1, 1972, pp. 407-412.

Shakespeare, William. "Let the bird of loudest lay" (*The Phoenix and the Turtle*). *The Complete Sonnets and Poems*, edited by Colin Burrow, Oxford University Press, 2002, lines 25–28.

———. *The Most Excellent and Lamentable Tragedie of Romeo and Iuliet. Newly Corrected, Augmented, and Amended.* Cuthbert Burby, 1599. Sig. B4v–Cr.

Singer, Natasha. "Scouring the Web to Make New Words 'Lookupable.'" *The New York Times*, 4 Oct. 2015, sec. BU, p. 3.

Stamper, Kory. *Word by Word*. Vintage, 2017.

Taub, Moshe. *Jews in the New World: History, Halachah, and Hashkafa*. Mosaica Press, 2024.

Tolkien, J.R.R. *The Hobbit*. George Allen & Unwin, 1937.

Tras, Zeliha, Merve Gül Sunbul, and Umay Bilge Baltaci. "Investigation of the Relationship Between Optimism, Perceived Social Support, and Hope." *i.e.: Inquiry in Education*, vol. 13, no. 1, 2021, article 11. *Digital Commons*.

About the Editor

Ibid, better known as ibid-11962, is a specialist in the Wizarding World, particularly in the different sources of canon, as well as a cataloguer of the various editions and versions of J.K. Rowling's writings, manuscripts, illustrations, and more. He has been active for over a decade in various forums and social networks, including *The Harry Potter Lexicon* and Reddit, where he shares his categorization, commentary, and discoveries. He is a long-time collaborator of *The Rowling Library*, and this book, *The Phoenix or The Flame*, is his first published work on *Harry Potter*. When he's not researching and reading about *Harry Potter*, he pursues scholarship on the works of Christopher Paolini and J.R.R. Tolkien.

Published by TRL Books:

Secret History of the Wizarding Phenomenon

The Phoenix or the Flame

www.ingramcontent.com/pod-product-compliance
Ingram Content Group UK Ltd.
Pitfield, Milton Keynes, MK11 3LW, UK
UKHW030759030325
4824UKWH00012B/89

9 798897 667932